D1048837

~LITTAUER LIBRARY, HARVARD UNIVERSITY~

JAN 1 4 2002

Where Now for New Labour?

The Fabian Society

The Fabian Society has played a central role for more than a century in the development of political ideas and public policy on the left of centre. Analysing the key challenges facing the UK and the rest of the industrialized world in a changing society and global economy, the Society's programme aims to explore the political ideas and the policy reforms which will define progressive politics in the new century.

The Society is unique among think-tanks in being a democratically constituted membership organization. It is affiliated to the Labour Party but is editorially and organizationally independent. Through its publications, seminars and conferences, the Society provides an arena for open-minded public debate.

FABIAN
S O C I E T Y

Policy Network

Policy Network is an organization that aims to link and inform those involved in progressive policies and ideas. It is the accelerating pace of change that makes it necessary for governments to learn from the experience of policies tried and tested by others and to strive to identify best practice. Policy Network aims to link together what can often be highly distinct national policy debates and it encourages those leading the development of progressive government policy to explore their ideas with some of the leading commentators and experts from around the world.

Working closely with governments and policy-makers in more than twenty-five countries, it provides a range of tools to help people work together and to keep the public in touch with innovations. The Policy Network website, www.policy-network.net, is a unique source of news and analysis for people with a serious interest in progressive ideas and politics.

policy network

JN
1129.32
.G4
2002

Where Now for New Labour?

Anthony Giddens

Polity

Copyright © Anthony Giddens 2002

The right of Anthony Giddens to be identified as author of this work has been asserted in accordance with the Copyright, Designs and Patents Act 1988.

First published in 2002 by Polity Press, The Fabian Society and Policy Network in association with Blackwell Publishers Ltd

Editorial office:
Polity Press
65 Bridge Street
Cambridge CB2 1UR, UK

Marketing and production:
Blackwell Publishers Ltd
108 Cowley Road
Oxford OX4 1JF, UK

Published in the USA by
Blackwell Publishers Inc.
350 Main Street
Malden, MA 02148, USA

Fabian Society
11 Dartmouth Street
London SW1H 9BN
www.fabian-society.org.uk

Policy Network
Elizabeth House
39 York Road
Waterloo
London SE1 7NQ
www.policy-network.net

All rights reserved. Except for the quotation of short passages for the purposes of criticism and review, no part of this publication may be reproduced, stored in a retrieval system, or transmitted, in any form or by any means, electronic, mechanical, photocopying, recording or otherwise, without the prior permission of the publisher.

Except in the United States of America, this book is sold subject to the condition that it shall not, by way of trade or otherwise, be lent, re-sold, hired out, or otherwise circulated without the publisher's prior consent in any form of binding or cover other than that in which it is published and without a similar condition including this condition being imposed on the subsequent purchaser.

A catalogue record for this book is available from the British Library.

Library of Congress Cataloging-in-Publication Data

Giddens, Anthony.
    Where now for New Labour? / Anthony Giddens.
        p.   cm.
    ISBN 0-7456-2991-1 (alk. paper)
    1. Labour Party (Great Britain)   2. Great Britain—Politics and government—1997–   I. Title.
    JN1129.L32 G53 2002
    324.24107—dc21
                                                                2001007340

LITTAUER LIBRARY
NORTH YARD
HARVARD UNIVERSITY
AUG 0 6 2002

Typeset in 11 on 14 pt Sabon
by Ace Filmsetting Ltd, Frome, Somerset
Printed in Great Britain by MPG Books, Bodmin, Cornwall

This book is printed on acid-free paper.

Contents

Preface

I started writing this work in August 2001 and finished it in early November. When I began, it was evident that the economic climate was becoming more and more uncertain. Since then the terrorist attacks of September 11, 2001 in the United States and their aftermath have injected yet more volatility into the world situation.

No one knows what will come next, or what the impact of these developments on the UK will be. It seems clear that there is an economic recession in the US and that at this moment it is deepening. The British economy will feel the effects and the country as a whole must adjust to a future that has become more imponderable than before. But while we cannot say where events will lead over the next few months, I hope I have provided an analysis of the prospects for New Labour that will prove accurate and robust. The policies introduced by the Labour government thus far have helped strengthen the social and economic institutions of the country. As a result Britain should be well placed to weather whatever challenges there are to come.

I should like to thank a number of people who read early versions of the manuscript and gave me critical comments, quite often hard-hitting ones. As he has so often been before, David Held was an invaluable source of help and encouragement. Michael Jacobs, of the Fabian Society, wrote extended critiques of the two first drafts,

Preface

from which I learned a great deal and to which I hope I have responded adequately. Andrew Adonis, George Jones, Denise Annett and Neil Stewart offered further extremely useful criticisms and comments. I have learned a lot over the past two years from conversations with Will Hutton and David Marquand, even if we do not always agree with one another. Nicky Short provided me with excellent research assistance, while Miriam Clarke was an enormous source of help in correcting the various drafts. Anne de Sayrah, as always, played an essential part. I would also like to thank Frederic Michel from the Policy Network, Ann Bone, Sue Leigh and all the staff at Polity who have been efficient and helpful throughout.

Anthony Giddens
London School of Economics and Political Science
November 28, 2001

Introduction

Not long ago the journalist John Lloyd had the temerity to write that 'this has been the best Labour government of the past half century.'[1] He was severely lambasted for his pains, as he must have known would happen – not from the right, but from the left. The response was entirely predictable. It has become the orthodoxy in the left-of-centre press to say that New Labour is all sound-bite and no substance, that it has lost touch with its social democratic roots and has abandoned the traditional leftist concern with redistribution.

Labour's 'third way' comes in for the sharpest attacks of all, even from those who are otherwise well disposed towards the New Labour project. In February 2001 Tony Blair put his name to an article in *Prospect* magazine called 'The third way, phase two'. It drew a ferocious response from the journalist Polly Toynbee, writing in the *Guardian*. Blair's 'third way, phase two', Toynbee said, 'is a useless road map for present policy'. The third way 'is now utterly redundant'. It is in any case 'an escape from self-definition – a butterfly always on the wing', a philosophy that has no essential core because 'it temptingly offers the best of all possible worlds'.[2]

In the following discussion I shall seek to defend New Labour against such criticisms, many of which are ill-founded. The attitude of the left to the third way debate in the UK is quite different from elsewhere. In recent years I have been to many countries talking about this debate and have met a variety of political leaders in the process. I don't think I've been to one where the discussion is as ill informed or dogmatic as it generally is here. I shall look into why this is the case, and try to provide a more accurate account of the strengths and limitations of the New Labour project. While I am critical of many of the critics, I think Labour can develop a more effective ideological and policy position than has been achieved thus far – and can also thereby more effectively cope with new developments in the wider world.

1

New Labour and its Critics

The left's disinclination to take the third way debate seriously and its disillusionment with New Labour are clearly linked. Of course, every leftist party in power finds itself criticized by many of its erstwhile supporters for not being left-wing enough. But in this case there is something more going on – a wilful refusal to face up to the changes the left must make to adapt to the world in which we find ourselves. On this topic, many on the British left are in a state of denial.

Why should this be so? I would sum up the reasons as follows – *insularity*, *memory loss*, *intellectual laziness*, and what one might call *the Groucho Marx tendency*.

Insularity

Most political discussion in this country, especially in the media, takes place almost completely outside a comparative context. Consider again the third way debate. From what is written about this debate in Britain, one would get no sense that it is a worldwide phenomenon, or that almost all centre-left parties have restructured their doctrines in response to it. Looking at the European party scene, the respected German political scientist Wolfgang Merkel rightly observes that 'the debate about the third way has become the most important reform discourse in the European party landscape.'[3] There are a variety of third ways rather than a single one, since countries have different political traditions, while governments mostly operate in coalitions and have to cope with varying types of interest groups in forging concrete policy programmes.

Merkel distinguishes four third ways among EU social democratic parties: the New Labour model, the 'polder model' in the Netherlands, the 'reformed welfare state path' in Sweden and the 'statist path' of the French socialists. Centre-left parties in other EU countries tend to approximate in their policies to one or other of these positions.

The 'polder model' is closest to the programme of New Labour. It is widely accepted as perhaps the most successful policy mix in Europe. In the late 1980s the Dutch economy was in poor shape, while the welfare system was creaking. Reforms were introduced to reduce high levels of state debt, combined with tax reductions to stimulate investment and encourage job creation. Cuts were made in some areas of social security and measures introduced to increase labour market flexibility. The welfare state in the Netherlands remains strong and has been combined with good economic growth and high levels of employment. In 1985 the employment ratio (the proportion of the available labour force in jobs) in Holland was only 52 per cent. By 2000 it stood at over 75 per cent.

Some thirty years ago Sweden was regarded as the social democratic state *par excellence* by most sympathetic observers. The country had a highly developed welfare system, based on universal benefits, full employment and a consensual incomes policy. The Swedish third way was born out of a series of crises the system faced over some twenty years, which reached their culmination in the early 1990s, when unemployment escalated and the country faced a huge budget deficit. A range of welfare reforms was introduced and cuts made in various social services. Taxes on business were reduced and there was a move away from direct taxation towards consumption taxes. Welfare reform has not gone as far in Sweden as in the Netherlands (or indeed the other Scandinavian countries, Denmark and Finland). The country has the lowest levels of income inequality of any EU country, but a price has been paid for this achievement. There has been a fall in workforce participation and the relative economic prosperity of the country has declined – suggesting that further change is called for.

More than any other centre-left party in Europe, the French socialists seem to have rejected the third way, and certainly want to have nothing to do with the term itself. Lionel Jospin famously set out his position as 'yes to a market economy, no to a market society'. Alone among European social democrats, the French government introduced a policy to reduce the legal length of the working week, to thirty-five hours. The labour market otherwise remains largely unreformed. Have the French therefore discovered a means of keeping traditional doctrines intact, avoiding third way type policies? They have not. The socialists in France had already abandoned Keynesian economic policies in the 1980s, following Mitterrand's failed attempt to deploy them. Jospin's government has privatized larger segments of French industry than his conservative predecessors. The thirty-five-hour working week could be seen as a disguised instrument of labour market flexibility, since it is an average, counted across the year. Unemployment in France has come down, but to date still stands at over 9 per cent. The proportion of people in work is only 62 per cent, well under that needed if social benefits are to be sustainable at anything like their current levels.

Why is all this relevant to New Labour in this country? Such comparisons show that Labour is not arbitrarily discarding leftist traditions, but reacting to structural changes that every country faces. They also indicate that there are not unified and ideal policies that social democratic parties can follow – they must ponder trade-offs.

Memory loss

Today's leftist critics seem to have blanked out the past. At the opening of the 1990s Britain was the site of animated discussion on the left – largely because of the success of Thatcherism. Most recognized the need to break away from established leftist positions. After all, Labour had lost three elections in a row. Things are not nearly so lively now. Many people act almost as if the attempts to develop new thinking had never happened at all – as if Labour could somehow go back to the very policies that kept the party out of power for so long.

Again a comparative sense might help here. Britain was not the only country where the left found itself in the doldrums in the 1980s and early 1990s. Across Europe, as well as in the US, social democracy was largely out of fashion and out of power. In some countries, such as Italy, the left had never governed at all. One only has to go back to the literature of the time to see how pessimistic most on the centre-left were. The sociologist Ralf Dahrendorf (himself a liberal) spoke of the 'end of the social democratic century'. He meant that social democracy was locked into an inevitable decline, because the programmes of the left had lost most of their popular appeal. Many on the left seemed to accept such a diagnosis themselves. In his conclusion to a volume on the state of social democracy in Europe, published in 1993, Richard Gillespie spoke of the 'air of disappointment that has surrounded social democratic renewal'. He attributed this situation to 'the immensity of the problems with which these parties are dealing'.[4] In common with Labour in this country, most centre-left parties fared poorly in elections in the early 1990s.

The social democratic revival arguably began in the very year Gillespie's book was in the course of production, 1992, with the election of Bill Clinton to the US presidency. Clinton was the first Democrat in the White House for twelve years (he was also the first to achieve re-election for a full second term since Roosevelt in 1936).

Nevertheless, the renewed success of social democracy took most people by surprise. When Tony Blair got into power, closely followed by Lionel Jospin, Gerhard Schröder and the Olive Tree coalition in Italy, the authors of a follow-up volume to that of Gillespie spoke wonderingly of 'the magical return of social democracy'.[5] Just as in the UK, however, these successes only followed programmatic renewal. The Clintonite Democrats, of course, were the model for New Labour. On an ideological level, Clinton's break with the Democratic past was dramatic:

> A party that for the past thirty years had been seen as profligate 'tax and spenders', reflexive defenders of federal government programmes, pacifist isolationists and advocates of an active social liberalism [in the US sense] now had a president who championed the reinvention of government, welfare reform, fiscal restraint, economic growth, free trade, mainstream values, and an internationalist foreign policy.[6]

Yet policy change was the order of the day for continental centre-left parties as well. The various 'third ways' just mentioned were the outcome of conscious endeavours to break with old-style social democracy. In Germany, for example, where the social democrats (SPD) had been out of power for almost as long as Labour, five years of intensive discussion led to radical shifts of view from the past. The SPD recognized that its ethos of solidarity no longer commanded support among the 'affluent majority'. The state was henceforth only to set the 'framework conditions' for economic activity,

7

which necessarily would be driven by the 'autonomous decisions of entrepreneurs'. Social democrats must now emphasize freedom of choice and equality of opportunity rather than the more traditional forms of state provision and egalitarianism.

Reversing years of social democratic decline was a painful and difficult business. The ideological and policy-making gains that were made then should not be forgotten, but built upon. We need to continue to go forward from them, not try to go back to the future.

Intellectual laziness

This trait is closely bound up with the other two. It consists of substituting easy assertion for hard analysis, particularly where there are trade-offs to be dealt with. Roy Hattersley, reborn as the scourge of New Labour, recently declared that Labour 'is no longer my party', since 'Tony Blair's dream of a meritocratic Britain is not the dream of a true social democrat.'[7] Equality of opportunity should not have a prime place in the social democratic lexicon, which must favour large-scale redistribution. Moreover, New Labour has substituted an anodyne term, 'social exclusion', for what the left should really be concerned with, which is poverty.

Now the redistribution of income, wealth and life chances certainly should remain a core part of what Labour stands for. But it is foolish to suppose we can ignore the difficult trade-offs that we face when tackling inequality. A comparative perspective is once more useful here, since it shows that the problems involved are in no sense peculiar to the UK.

Consider, for example, the dilemmas social democrats must grapple with concerning inequality and employment. As of early 2001, about 10 per cent of the EU labour force, some 15 million people, were unemployed. Were the EU states to match the employment ratio of the US at that date, 30 million more, twice the number registered as unemployed, would be in work. There is no hope of generating more jobs without expansion in the service sector. Low-end services are very price sensitive. If we rule out American-style deregulation, what options are there?

The most acute analyst of these issues, sociologist Gøsta Esping-Anderson, argues that there is a win–win welfare model for social democrats, but only if we are prepared to accept a different version of equality from that traditionally favoured by the left – essentially an opportunity-based view.[8] The service sector can create many new jobs, but it cannot guarantee that they will all be good ones. We need to ensure that, as far as possible, people do not get trapped in the poorest-paid jobs, but have the chance of mobility upwards. This goal means giving priority to social investment – such as training and retraining schemes – rather than to traditional passive re-distribution, as Hattersley proposes. Such schemes can be fruitfully integrated with tax credits for low-paid workers and with targeted policies to combat social exclusion. This strategy is in fact deployed by the EU countries that have managed to combine high levels of employment with effective social protection, such as the Netherlands, Denmark – and the UK under New Labour.

A focus upon social exclusion has nothing to do with trying to sweep poverty under the carpet. The phrase 'social exclusion' was not invented by New Labour, but by social scientists, who have pointed to the range of factors that prevent the worse-off from participating in the wider society. The class structure of Western societies has altered fundamentally over the last thirty years. The main concern of the left in previous generations was the integration of the manual working class into the wider society. And that working class was large: not that long ago, some 40 per cent of the workforce was in blue-collar, manual labour. Now well under half that number are. Today, in a much more affluent society than in the past, the key social and economic problems concern the divisions that have opened up between the bottom 5–10 per cent of the population and the rest. Social exclusion is not just about poverty, but about living in neighbourhoods that are crime-ridden and lack access to shops, transport, decent schooling and job opportunities. Many of the excluded are to some degree casualties of the welfare state itself, caught up in a negative spiral of welfare dependency.

The Groucho Marx tendency

Groucho declared that he wouldn't want to join any club that would have him as a member. The Groucho Marx tendency in politics is the view that anything that can actually be achieved in the sphere of orthodox democratic politics by definition can't be worthwhile, and therefore should be either scorned or ignored. It is a classic manoeuvre of the far left, and deeply embedded in its history. But other leftists also flirt with it. Many on the left have always thought they know better than citizens what is good for them – hence the authoritarian traits that have long dogged leftist thinking.

The Groucho Marx tendency is alive and well among some of the critics of New Labour. It shades over into the difficulties the left has long had with the realities of power and with the compromises that being in government entails. For most of the past century, in most of the industrial countries, the left has more often been out of rather than in power. Idealism can more easily be preserved when one is on the outside looking in. Some on the left undoubtedly are happier when there is a government of the right rather than one of the left, where enemies can more easily be attacked and ideological integrity more readily maintained.

Those who have succumbed to the Groucho Marx tendency have a worse case of memory loss than their counterparts on the more moderate left. They act as though 1989 had never happened, and as if Cold War ideological positions could still be maintained. Yet socialism is dead as a theory of economic management. The driving force of socialism, in its many varieties, was the idea that a consciously controlled economy would be superior to market capitalism. This core notion has proved to be false. No market system can work effectively or equitably without regulation and without the active intervention of government. But to pretend or imply that there is a known alternative to the market economy is a delusion.

Since some of the difficulties the third way debate has experienced in this country might arise from the term itself, I shall speak more often in what follows of the 'new social democracy' or the 'new centre-left'. As I define it, the new social democracy has two main characteristics. First, it recognizes the need for a profound rethinking of leftist doctrines in the light of the big changes happening in the world. Whereas ten years ago there was more of an inchoate awareness of change, there is more consensus among social scientists and political thinkers now about what these big changes are: globalization (in spite of the controversies about it, now much better understood), the emergence of the knowledge economy, the rise of individualism and 'postmaterialist' concerns, the dysfunctions of the welfare state and the emergence of new risks, especially those linked to climate change and the environment.

Second, the new social democracy concentrates upon the conditions necessary to achieve electoral success. This perspective does not imply rejecting idealism. It does mean addressing the real concerns of voters rather than opting for an impotent ideological purity. Now that its traditional base of support, the working class, has shrunk so much, to come even close to government any left-of-centre party must appeal to a wide cross-class constituency. With the 'magical return' of social democracy, social democratic

11

governments, or coalitions in which social democrats dominate, are in power in eleven out of the fifteen EU countries. But there is little or no evidence of a generic turn towards the more traditional left. Parties that stick to an old left agenda, or something close to it, favouring statism and heavy redistribution, get no more than 9 per cent voting support in any EU state. Social democratic parties, in fact, on average have less than 30 per cent voting support across Europe, and in most cases support is stronger among older than among younger voters (New Labour is an exception on both counts).

The electoral revival of the left has a tenuous basis. New Labour gained a larger proportion of the vote in the 1997 and 2001 elections than any other left-of-centre party in Europe – and this was only just over 40 per cent. By contrast, the French socialists only achieved 23 per cent of the vote when Lionel Jospin came to power. Virtually every centre-left party or coalition in power in the EU did so in circumstances where either the right was split or fragmented, or where there had been a long period of rightist government and voters wanted a change. The SPD and green coalition won in Germany, for instance, partly because voters became disenchanted after a long period of Christian Democratic rule.

Political surveys in this country and elsewhere show that the ideological changes made by social democratic parties – in this country, the shift from Old to New Labour – were crucially important in persuading key categories of voters to switch their votes. But centre-left parties will have to continue to think tactically as well as sharpening up their ideas and policies. The majority of voters in all Western democracies are now politically 'dealigned' – they have no clear and continuing commitment to any party.

This trend is especially noticeable in two-party systems. The recent book, *The Radical Centre*, by Fred Halstead and Michael Lind, shows that today 42 per cent of Americans describe themselves as independents, far more than are affiliated to either the Democrats or the Republicans.[9] In the UK, 50 per cent of voters describe themselves as neither left nor right, but as moderates. The proportion is about the same in Germany, France and Italy. A national poll during the 2000 election in the US showed that under 20 per cent described themselves as 'liberals' (that is, social democrats in the European sense) and only 29 per cent as 'conservatives'.[10]

The ever-growing influence of the media also promotes dealignment. The media increasingly structure the framework of politics. Politicians must respond on a daily basis to media stories. Political life more and more takes the form of a continuous dialogue between politicians and the citizenry, filtered through the media. According to some, a new form of direct democracy is emerging, in which political leaders are continually on trial, but where they also have the advantage of being able to communicate directly with the public.[11] However that may be, this situation undoubtedly injects a further volatility into the political scene. Voters have become used to picking and choosing. Brand loyalty in the sphere of consumption counts for much less than in the past. Voters more and more have a calculative attitude to politics too.

2

Myths of the Left

The attitudes mentioned above have helped create a number of pervasive myths about the new social democracy and its relevance to the UK. One I shall call the myth of *incoherence*, the second the myth of *orthodox social democracy* and the third the myth of *taxation*.

The myth of incoherence

The myth of incoherence is well represented in Polly Toynbee's remarks, but many others could have been quoted to the same effect, since this view is so widely held and often repeated. Polly Toynbee talks of a butterfly always on the wing. Others have compared the third way to the Loch Ness Monster: much talked about, but never seen. In fact, there is at least as much coherence and integration to the centre-left now as there was at any point in the past – almost certainly more so if one looks across social democratic parties in the EU, as Donald Sassoon has pointed out.[12]

In his discussion Merkel concentrates upon the differences between the main social democratic perspectives in Europe, but just as obvious is what they have in common. There is a clear overall framework for the new social democratic politics, and its main

Myths of the Left

features can easily be stated. The new social democracy seeks to preserve the basic values of the left – a belief in a solidary and inclusive society, a commitment to combating inequality and protecting the vulnerable. It asserts that active government, coupled with strong public institutions and a developed welfare state, have an indispensable role to play in furthering these objectives. But it holds that many traditional leftist perspectives or policies either no longer do so, or have become directly counterproductive.

The main elements of such a framework are:

(1)   Reform of the state, not in order to diminish public institutions and services, but to renew and enhance them. The public interest is often best served where the state collaborates with other agencies, including non-profit organizations, business, and third sector groups.

The state can sometimes act to undermine the public interest rather than sustain it. This is where the Old Left went wrong. State agencies do not promote the public interest wherever they are too unwieldy, bureaucratic, driven by producer interests, or operate with soft budget constraints. Structural reform of the public services is required to make them more effective and more responsive to citizens' needs.

(2)   The maintaining of fiscal discipline and a balanced budget across the economic cycle. 'Tax and spend' for leftist parties in the past didn't normally mean what it says – it meant 'tax and overspend'. Left-of-centre parties habitually entered into spending commitments they couldn't afford and sometimes ran up massive state debts in the process. Some EU countries, such as Belgium in the late 1980s, found themselves paying out as much as 10 per cent of GDP per annum on interest payments to fund welfare obligations.

It won't do to think of taxation only in relation to social justice.

Fiscal policies almost always have consequences for economic be-haviour, and hence for competitiveness, which must be borne in mind in policy formation. Social policy and economic policy need to be connected, not treated as though they were in separate com-partments. Welfare policies almost always have economic conse-quences, while fiscal measures usually have a variety of social effects.

Heavy-handed government intervention is a thing of the past. Government, however, must seek to offer sound macroeconomic steering, create conditions under which economic innovation can flourish, and provide concentrated investment in education and skills training, continuing across the lifespan.

(3)   Structural reform of the welfare state, needed to cope with its problems and insufficiencies. These difficulties include unsustain-able commitments (as in many industrial countries, but not the UK, in the area of pensions); welfare provisions that are suboptimal or perverse in their consequences – such as benefits that lock people out of decent jobs they could otherwise be in; new risk situations which established welfare systems may find it hard to cope with, such as increasing child poverty; combating moral hazard in wel-fare programmes; and repairing the damage where well-intentioned welfare policies went wrong, such as dealing with the problems produced by the housing estates built in the 1960s and 1970s.

Welfare reforms must stress responsibilities as well as rights, in order to encourage active citizenship as well as to reduce welfare dependency. Active labour market policies, such as Labour's New Deal, form one example of how this emphasis can be translated into concrete policy.

(4)   A new approach to inequality, placing the emphasis upon equality of opportunity. We must recognize the difficulties and trade-offs involved in coping with inequalities, as well as the limited elec-

toral support that can be gained for direct redistribution of income to the poor. As mentioned earlier, changes in the class structure have to be addressed, and problems of social exclusion attacked in a direct way. Social exclusion is not just one form of poverty. There is no point simply transferring income to someone who cannot read the instructions on a medical bottle, or has a chronic drugs problem.

The best protection against poverty is holding a good job, and new social democrats rightly place a strong emphasis upon work. This perspective is not simply one advocated by New Labour. The slogan of the Dutch social democrats, for example, is 'work, work and work again'. Given a decent minimum wage threshold, a society that has a high employment ratio is in a far better welfare situation than one that does not. A high tax take can be generated, and the money spent on desired public goods rather than upon unemployment benefits.

(5)   A firm law and order orientation, recognizing that personal security ranks high on the list of most citizens' concerns. The motive for this stance is not, or should not be, an illiberal one. Freedom from the fear of crime is a major citizenship right, and one whose importance has been underestimated by the left in the past. Many leftists tended to treat crime as an artefact of inequality and poverty. There are close relationships between crime and deprivation, but some crimes, such as property crimes, increase with affluence (there is more to steal). In any case, criminality has to be addressed in the here and now.

(6)   A commitment to ecological modernization. Historically, ecological concerns have not had a high priority in social democratic parties. Part of the difficulty was, and is, that the social democratic orientation to economic growth and full employment is not easily

made compatible with environmental objectives. But the two can be brought much closer together than seemed possible in the past. Taxation can be a powerful means of furthering ecological goals, while it has become widely accepted that some environmentally sound practices and technologies can have positive effects upon both economic growth and job creation.

(7)   An international – or transnational – outlook, given concrete form in Europe by support for the EU and its expansion eastwards. We must 'take globalization seriously' – we have to accept that many policy questions cannot be dealt with, or opportunities grasped, only at the national or regional levels. This view does not imply taking an uncritical approach either to free trade or to the expansion of global market mechanisms. Regulation is needed, nationally and internationally, to promote corporate responsibility and control corporate power – and many other forms of international or transnational regulation or intervention are demanded too.

The myth of orthodox social democracy

While such a policy programme can no doubt be criticized, it is not incoherent. But is there an alternative version of social democracy that could be chosen to substitute for it? The idea that such a version exists is what I mean by the myth of *orthodox social democracy*. Many critics of New Labour propagate this myth. They have been harsh in their criticisms of Labour in power. David Marquand, for example, asks: 'Are Britain's Blairites social democrats?' And he answers: 'Yes, if you read their lips. No, if you watch their hands.'[13] He doesn't say exactly what he means by social democracy, but seems to have in mind a central European model of a social democratic state. Germany, France, and perhaps the Scandinavian countries, should be looked to if we are to understand what a valid social democratic state looks like. Since the early 1990s Will Hutton has pursued related themes in his book *The State We're In* and other publications.[14]

These arguments have the great virtue of being based on a comparative perspective. Moreover, no one could deny that the countries in question have a superior postwar record to the UK in terms of both economic development and a range of social criteria. There is much that can be learned in Britain from these successes. But the idea that there is some more valid version of social democracy that can be extracted from such comparisons and applied as a model for the present day does not stand up to scrutiny. It isn't accidental that social democratic parties in these countries have been following their own 'third ways', just like New Labour in the UK.

What brings success in one era doesn't necessarily do so in another. Moreover, when we compare countries, it won't do merely to look at what happened in the past. We have to look at current trajectories of development. Studies of these issues do not make encouraging reading for anyone who thinks the 'central European model' can still be a useful guide to the future. Its core problem is an inability to generate sufficient jobs.

The German expert on the welfare state and economic development, Fritz Scharpf, studied trends in the evolution of employment ratios in Europe and came up with some sobering conclusions. He looked at thirteen industrial countries over the period from 1970 to 1998.

In the EU only Denmark managed to sustain a high employment level throughout, and has moved to an even higher plane in recent years. The UK's level of employment fell during the 1980s, but recovered in the 1990s. In Sweden the rate peaked in the 1980s and subsequently became sharply reduced. The central European countries, such as Austria, Belgium, Germany and France, show a specific pattern. They started out in 1970 at the same level as other industrial states, but since then have shown a continuous decline. Significantly, the OECD's index of labour market flexibility correlates closely with these differences, and with the changes over time.

As Scharpf makes clear, in the central European economies 'the problem is structural rather than conjunctural, and a bit more economic growth will not solve it.'[15] The continental welfare states do not support large numbers of public sector jobs (as Sweden does), nor do they generate jobs in the non-state sector. In the service sector they are especially weak. They therefore face in an acute way the dilemma noted earlier. Their regulated labour markets protect those in jobs, but make it hard for those from the outside to get in, creating insider/outsider labour markets. At the same time such labour markets tend to hamper business innovation and adaptation to technological change. Moreover, as measured by current trends rather than previous periods, these countries are not superior in terms of reducing economic inequalities.

Some are now introducing changes. In France, for example, an employment bonus (*Prime pour l'emploi*) is being introduced, which will be delivered through the fiscal system. It is a close cousin of Labour's New Deal.

We can say with some confidence that no feasible alternative model to the reformed social democratic one exists, at least at the present moment. We should be debating the limits and possibilities of this framework rather than pretending a more authentic one can be found.

The myth of taxation

It has become something of a mantra among leftist critics of New Labour to argue that public services in the UK are weaker than in most other EU states because taxation is too low as a proportion of GDP. This idea is what I call the myth of *taxation*. The thesis is not wholly wrong, but is only a half-truth. In so far as Britain's public institutions are in fact much worse than elsewhere (itself an issue that needs looking at), this situation also stems from the poor economic record of the country from the 1950s to the 1980s, and from the organizational and managerial weaknesses that underlay it.

The myth of taxation is an important legitimating device for critics of New Labour. It suggests a simple solution to the country's problems: raise taxes – the traditional approach of the left in any case. And it skirts an embarrassing issue for many leftists, the fact that Thatcherism scored some notable successes. Mrs Thatcher did not succeed in reducing the overall tax burden, but she did alter the pattern of taxation, reducing the top rate of income tax, lowering taxes on business, and placing more emphasis on consumption taxes. Britain's relative economic decline was halted during the Thatcher years and there is no point pretending that the reforms she introduced – in taxation and in other areas – were not part of the cause of this improvement. The UK was 'the sick man of Europe' for some thirty years from the 1950s to the late 1980s. By the opening of the 1990s the country was putting in a much stronger economic performance, and by 1995 the UK had pulled up to level terms with France in terms of prosperity per capita and was just behind Germany. Its manufacturing productivity continued to lag behind both, but had also substantially improved. Germany, for example, had a 47 per cent lead over the UK in manufacturing productivity in 1979. By 1996 this lead had been reduced to 26 per cent.

It was the proper strategy, therefore, for New Labour to keep some of Mrs Thatcher's reforms in place, including labour market reforms. Labour was also right to break away from the simple equation that higher tax rates equals better public services and more social justice. Each of these aims can sometimes be facilitated by tax rate reductions rather than tax increases. They are also affected by the relationship between taxation patterns and economic performance. Taxation cannot be tucked away under the 'social justice' label, as though it had no implications for economic activity. Yet leftist authors still often write as if there were no such implications. In November 2000, for instance, the Fabian Society published a lengthy book making recommendations about 'a new politics of tax for public spending'. In a large volume of 388 pages, only a few paragraphs made reference to relationships between fiscal mechanisms and economic growth.[16]

The tax take is crucially influenced by the employment ratio. Fiscal measures that help put and keep people in jobs can generate a higher tax take without tax increases. Although helped by a favourable economic environment, Labour in its first term generated a large surplus of money available to be spent on public services. Some writers speak as though this outcome was just a lucky accident, but it was in large part the result of policy innovation. Labour was able to emulate what was achieved in the US under the Clinton administration, where a large budget surplus was generated – which the Democrats proposed to devote mainly to social spending.

In making these points I do not mean to say that Labour should never consider raising tax rates. Moreover, the question of what proportion of GDP is needed to provide effectively for social needs merits serious discussion. But analysis of such issues must always bear in mind the need to reconcile social justice with an energetic and competitive economy. I take it that this recognition is one of the defining features of New Labour. One could say that the two pre-existing political philosophies – the old left and Thatcherism – were 'half theories'. Old Labour was strong on social justice, but was never successful in fostering a dynamic and competitive economy. Thatcherism was strong on competitiveness, but had virtually no account of social justice at all. New Labour must seek to reconcile the two, recognizing the difficult trade-offs that have to be confronted.

John Lloyd is right in his assessment of New Labour – as should be apparent to anyone not too afflicted by the various traits I referred to at the beginning. Labour is not only in power for a second term, with a majority almost as large as it enjoyed in the first. It is in the strongest position of any centre-left party in the EU. The low turnout in the 2001 election did not suggest that the citizenry has embraced Labour with massive enthusiasm. But nowhere else in Europe has any left-of-centre party or leader generated such ardour either. This is part of the temper of the age, in which voters tend to take a muted and instrumental approach to political choice.

Labour's first term

Various detailed analyses of Labour's first term exist, and I shall not seek to duplicate them here.[17] My brief checklist would be as follows. (I differentiate between 'clear successes' and 'half-way houses' but the boundary between these is not clear-cut. Moreover, the 'successes' are all less than complete, with much more still to accomplish.)

Successes

(1) Marginalizing the Tories, perhaps even in an enduring way. It is important to recognize that the travails of the Conservatives are not just of their own making, but come from the switch from Old to New Labour. New Labour took over from the Democrats the idea that political opponents should not be able to 'own' any issues. A centre-left party must seek to outflank the right on

questions of economic competence, fiscal discipline, defence and law and order, fields where the right has always been strong, not just keep ahead in its 'homeland' areas of social welfare, education, health and poverty.

(2)   Economic policy. Labour has been successful in gaining the confidence of the electorate as the party best equipped to run the economy. Unlike previous Labour governments – *all* previous Labour governments – this one did not succumb to an economic crisis after a few years in power. New Labour was much criticized for sticking for the first two years to the tight spending limits designated by the previous government. Yet it was the condition of the surplus generated later. Previous Labour governments had spent early on, only to find themselves unable to meet their commitments subsequently. New Labour has also fostered a constructive relationship with business. This shift was not easy to achieve. Labour faced prejudices in many business and City circles. It was a necessary endeavour, however, because it is not possible to run a successful market economy without the confidence and commitment of the major wealth-producers.

(3)   Welfare reform, or at least some aspects of it. The New Deal, the Working Families Tax Credit, child-care strategy and other innovations have proved their worth. Reform of the welfare system is a highly charged and difficult business, as all governments attempting it have found. The social rights accorded by the welfare state, once established, tend to be seen as natural rights, provoking fierce resistance to those who seek to change them. The government faced a furore, for example, when benefits for lone parents were reduced. Yet this reduction went along with offering increased opportunities and job training via the New Deal. Those societies where lone parents fare best, such as Denmark, are also ones where

the highest proportion is in work. In Denmark, this proportion amounts to fully 90 per cent, far higher than in the UK.

(4)   The fostering of a high employment economy, with a decent minimum wage and generous schemes for training and retraining. As of early 2001, the UK had an employment ratio of 75 per cent, one of the highest in Europe.

(5)   Redistribution – contrary to what the critics say. The tax reductions and credits introduced to 'make work pay' have achieved considerable success. According to independent studies Labour's policies lifted well over a million people out of poverty between 1997 and 2000. Depending upon wider economic conditions the existing schemes, plus further tax credits, such as the Children's Tax Credit now coming on-stream, should add substantially to this number.

According to figures of the Institute for Fiscal Studies the post-tax income of the average household in the bottom 10 per cent of income earners rose by 8.8 per cent over the period. The richest 30 per cent of households experienced a fall in post-tax income.[18]

Targeted pension increases, directed towards poorer retirees, should radically reduce the number of older people living in poverty within a short period of time. It will take longer before we know how effective other policies directed towards reducing poverty will be, but there are many such policies in play. They include longer-term programmes to do with the social and economic renewal of deprived areas, educational innovations, regional employment schemes, improved facilities for child care, community banking, micro-credit programmes and so forth.

(6)   Some key aspects of education policy. In a speech just before the 1997 election, Tony Blair set out no fewer than twenty-one

promises about the future of education. Among them were proposals to reduce class sizes, implement a literacy strategy, link all schools to the internet, set targets for improvement for every school and local authority, and close down failing schools. Major problems exist with some of these policies, and especially with higher education, but distinct improvements did occur in areas such as literacy and numeracy.

Half-way houses

(1)   Constitutional reform. Labour's constitutional reforms – especially the creation of the Scottish parliament, the Welsh Assembly and the Northern Ireland Assembly – have been substantial and have changed the country significantly. Yet they seem to have been driven as much by events as by ideological conviction. 'De facto devolution' was revealed in the 1997 election results, where the party that resisted change, the Tories, was left without any seats whatsoever in either Scotland or Wales. The Regional Development Agencies are effectively agencies of central government with some responsibilities for the regions. Reform of the House of Lords has passed only its first stage, while the Freedom of Information Act was restricted in scope. The conflict in Northern Ireland has been contained and muted, but a lasting peace remains to be established.

(2)   The National Health Service. Given its core importance to the public, Labour came into power with surprisingly few plans for restructuring the NHS, although some reforms were enacted very early on. Tony Blair seems to have been prompted in a TV interview to increase funding for the NHS to the 'European average'. Following this episode, there was widespread consultation with staff in the health service, leading to the publication of the NHS Plan in

July 2000. Tangible improvements so far, however, have been rather few, and in this key area – as in the reform of public services more generally – much remains to play for.

(3)   Crime and punishment. Labour has succeeded in replacing the Tories as the 'party of law and order', a basic aspect of widening its electoral appeal. The Crime and Disorder Act of 1998 was comprehensive, and included policies such as the fast sentencing of persistent young offenders, parenting and reparation orders, reduction of the age of criminal responsibility, and anti-social behaviour penalties. Large-scale funding has been allocated to occupational training, drugs treatment and counselling in prison. A focus upon reducing the causes of crime is an explicit part of the brief of the Social Exclusion Unit, set up in 1998. Yet Labour's policies continue to look disturbingly like those of the outgoing Tory government, with its defined streak of authoritarianism. The prison population, already the highest among the EU countries, continues to rise.

(4)   Relations with the European Union. New Labour has made considerable progress in bringing the UK closer to the 'heart of Europe', certainly as compared with preceding Tory governments. Labour ended the UK's opposition to the Social Chapter and signed up to various other EU initiatives. The government has sought to build new alliances and through them to influence policy. The support of Spain and Portugal, for instance, was important in the shaping of the Lisbon summit, which marked a significant shift of emphasis for the EU. A speech Tony Blair gave in Warsaw in October 2000 was the first time a British prime minister had set out a positive, wide-ranging view of the EU's future. Yet the fact that the UK has stayed out of the euro necessarily lessens its influence, and the government has done little thus far to move public opinion in a more favourable direction.

(5)   The environment. The 1997 manifesto stated that 'we will put concern for the environment at the heart of policy-making, so that it is not an add-on extra, but informs the whole of government.'[19] A range of positive innovations were made (described further below), certain of them very significant. Nevertheless, some of New Labour's biggest difficulties came in the environmental field, including the continuing problem of BSE, genetically modified crops, coping with abnormal weather patterns and floods, fuel protests and turmoil in the railway system.

Failures

(1)   The dismal saga of the dome.

(2)   PR and communications. Active media management originally was widely thought to be one of New Labour's strong points. But the whole approach not only rebounded, it severely damaged Labour's image in ways from which it has proved difficult to recover. New Labour became thought of as empty of content, as lacking in substantive policies – a perception far from the reality.

(3)   The promotion of corporate responsibility. As noted earlier, Labour has successfully cemented a good relationship with business. It has done little, however, to curb irresponsible business activity or corporate profiteering. Labour has not developed a policy framework relevant to corporate social responsibility, certainly not one with bite.

3

'Third Way, Phase Two'

New Labour has a second term in office, and could plausibly have a third. Tony Blair has rightly said that the second term cannot be just a rerun of the first, echoing the 'third way, phase two' theme. The 'first phase of New Labour was essentially one of reassurance – we weren't going to repeat the economic mistakes of the past . . . there would be no old-style tax and spend.' It is time for 'a second phase of New Labour, defined less by reference to the old Labour Party, than by an agenda for the country, radical but firmly in the centre ground, the ground we have made our own in the past few years.'[20] But what should this agenda be?

The new context

New Labour, like the new social democracy more generally, was created in a specific conjunction of circumstances, described earlier. They are no longer the same as they were. Bill Clinton has come and gone. In place of the New Democrats there is a Republican administration, which shares few of the ideas or perspectives of its predecessor. Labour could find itself more isolated in Europe, given that most of the social democratic governments in the EU are not in an especially strong electoral position. Moreover, a renewed

29

polarization of political life is now visible. On the one hand there is the anti-globalization movement, at least some members of which are on the anti-capitalist left. On the other, there is the rise of a new radical right in many countries, which is also hostile to globalization. These groups and parties cover a range of different views. But they also have some common themes, principally an emphasis upon the preservation of national identity and power, coupled to economic protectionism. Each sees parliamentary democracy as essentially empty and unresponsive to citizens' needs. Both are prepared to take direct action, in a minority of cases violent action, to pursue their concerns.

When the 'magical return' of social democracy first got under way, the economic climate was favourable. The US enjoyed years of unprecedented growth, coupled to high employment levels and low inflation. Between 1992 and 1999 GDP in the US grew by 24 per cent. The average for the EU over the same period was only 15 per cent, although this figure conceals wide variations. The US is currently in the grip of an economic downturn, the likely duration and severity of which are unknown. The major EU economies may show higher rates of growth over the next two or three years than the US, but they have a long way to go to close the gap. The EU states are being pulled down by the deteriorating economy in the US. If the EU economies, or some of them, can outstrip the US over the next few years, it will not be by much. On top of all this there have been the terrorist attacks in New York and Washington, and the military response of the US and its allies, with all the political and economic uncertainties they have brought in their wake. The 'third way, phase two' must respond to this altered climate, and to the limitations of its pre-existing policies.

Much of the framework elaborated during the first term can and should remain intact. Labour must continue to situate itself firmly on the centre ground of politics, and avoid defining itself as a party of sectional or class interests. The contemporary centre-left should reject the old left's conception of itself as a class-based force in society. This point is fundamental because it means we can overcome the barrier that used to exist between the left and liberal progressivism, one of the defining features of the new social democracy.

The need to connect economic and social policy remains every bit as important in an economic downturn as it was in a more favourable economic climate. The commitment to sustainable financing across the economic cycle – the so-called 'golden rule' – should remain central to government expenditure. Responsible economic management of this sort has key advantages over a traditional leftist orientation to tax and spend. Money is not dissipated on interest repayments or on paying out unemployment benefits to people who could be in jobs at or above the minimum wage. Financial markets will not tend to react adversely to a country facing up to a weaker economic environment if these elements are in place, even when shocks occur. Circumstances were quite different in Britain in the last two world economic downturns of some ten and twenty years ago. In each of them the UK fared poorly as compared with most other industrial countries. Today Britain should be able to adapt better than almost any other developed economy, having achieved good growth rates combined with low inflation and sound public finances.

Labour has pushed the overall tax take to some 40 per cent of GDP, while reducing more taxes than have been increased. According to the Institute for Fiscal Studies between 1996–7 and 2000–1 government revenue rose by 2.9 per cent of GDP, from 37.6 per cent to 40.5 per cent.[21] For reasons already given, the relation between taxation and public goods is complex.[22] An optimum level of tax as a proportion of GDP for the country – one that balances the conditions for economic efficiency with the effective funding of public goods – would probably be higher, but there seems little chance of elevating the tax take much further, especially in a deteriorating economic environment. Taxpayers adjust their lifestyles to existing tax levels at any one point in time, and will resist more than relatively marginal changes. Scharpf's studies in fact show remarkable stability in the differences between tax levels in the EU countries over the past thirty years, suggesting resistance to major changes either up or down.

To keep the tax take at current levels in weakening economic circumstances may at some future point mean increases in formal tax rates. Gordon Brown signalled such a possibility in his pre-Budget speech of November 27, 2001. But there may be other means that could be deployed first of all – such as looking further at tax exemptions and allowances. Hypothecated taxes, less developed in the UK than in several other EU countries – particularly for NHS funding – might also play a part.[23] They have well-known difficulties, but have the great advantage of connecting tax directly to a clear social purpose.

Labour's welfare reforms should stand the government in good stead in a period of economic downturn. Its emphases upon education, employability and active labour market policies should help rather than hinder. An educated and adaptable labour force is more of an asset when economic prospects are weak than when they are not. Critics argue that the New Deal becomes an expensive irrelevance in such circumstances. For what is the point of training people for work when there are no jobs to go to? However, active labour market schemes have a proven track record in continental countries, including in times of economic downswing. In such circumstances, those with few or no skills are even more disadvantaged than in other periods. Experience from Sweden shows that active labour market policies do not prevent high unemployment when economic conditions are poor, but they do guard against large numbers of people becoming permanently unemployable.

The main challenges for New Labour are to:

1 develop its ideological thinking further, to progress beyond the ideas taken over from the New Democrats, and to respond to the transformations in the wider sociopolitical environment;
2 set out more clearly its project for the kind of society Britain should become;
3 build environmental thinking more centrally into its core policies;
4 clarify and make count its programme for the revival of public institutions;
5 develop a coherent interpretation of the evolving international order and the appropriate place of Britain within it.

Ideology

In the early to mid-1990s, in common with other social democratic parties, Labour was casting around for an effective ideological position. At that point the party did not really have a developed programme. One of Tony Blair's main advisers has admitted that, even at the time Blair was elected leader, 'I could not claim to have anything approaching a coherent set of political ideas.'[24] The void was filled largely by appropriating ideas and policies from the New Democrats. Many of the perspectives that became central to Labour's revisionism originated in the work of the think-tank of the New Democrats, the Democratic Leadership Council. They included a self-conscious break with the party's past, symbolized by a name change; the determination to become 'the party of the mainstream'; a retreat from tax and spend; an emphasis upon 'opportunity, responsibility and community'; a stress upon responsibilities as well as rights in welfare reform, a 'hand up rather than a handout' in the DLC's favourite phrase; tax credit schemes to help poorer individuals and families; targeted anti-poverty and urban regeneration schemes, involving distinct 'action zones'; and a tough approach to crime and punishment. Most became part of the more general reconstruction of social democratic programmes worldwide. As I have argued above many of them were correct and necessary, and should stay in place.

However, the perspectives that lie behind them reflect the time and the society in which they were produced. When Bill Clinton spoke of 'the end of big government', he was speaking in the context of a country that has always been suspicious of power being concentrated at the federal level. In fact, big government has not come to an end, nor is it desirable that it should do so. Levels of government expenditure in the US and the EU countries over the past two decades have stopped increasing, but have not gone down. Moreover, the electorate in the UK has a more positive attitude towards the benefits of government than the electorate in the US. New Labour should be able to, and must, make a more sustained defence of public institutions than the New Democrats were able to achieve. The political language and concepts of the New Democrats were drawn from the North American milieu, which is culturally different from European social democracy. The appropriation by New Labour of US-style terms – the New Deal and so forth – opened the way for possible misunderstandings. It could seem as if New Labour were positioning itself against European social democracy, rather than converging with it. These usages helped to give open field to those who, wilfully or otherwise, would misrepresent Labour's standpoint.

New Labour needs to answer the criticism that, in its anxiety to avoid the interventionist traits of earlier Labour governments, it has simply succumbed to the power of markets. How should this be done without returning to an Old Labour outlook, which rightly has been discarded? I would suggest in the following way.

'Third Way, Phase Two'

As a social democratic party, Labour should recognize that markets have imperfections and failures that need to be corrected by active government. If left to their own devices, markets produce too much inequality, and too much insecurity. The task of government is to reduce these, and to provide resources that will allow individuals to cope with those that remain. Markets often tend to monopoly, a situation in which their key advantages for the public, lying in their competitive nature and the consumer choice that follows from it, are lost. Government intervention is necessary to counteract this tendency. Moreover, markets depend for their functioning upon a diversity of public goods that they themselves can't provide. These include a framework of law and core goods such as education, welfare, defence and health services.

A strong and effective state is needed to fulfil these tasks. However, *government*, the *state* and the *public interest* are not the same. The prime commitment of a left-of-centre government should be to advance the public interest. What counts as 'in the public interest' is in principle settled by procedures of democratic debate and scrutiny. All parties claim to act in the public interest, but social democrats should have their own definition of it. It is in the public interest that sectional interests don't dominate, that the rule of law and the protection of liberties it enshrines are guaranteed, that social exclusion and poverty are combated and the framework of democratic rights, which creates a public sphere, is protected and deepened.

However, states have their own imperfections, limitations and failures. Advancing the cause of public services and public institutions often means that government must confront the state, and seek to regulate and reform it. Western countries have become used to a state staffed by officials who are mostly reliable, trustworthy and non-corrupt. Such isn't the case in many other countries around the world, where the state can be actively the enemy of the public interest. Even where largely harnessed to the public good, state institutions may leave much to be desired in terms of their effectiveness, responsiveness and transparency.

We should not contrast the 'public' with the 'private' in the naïve way that is often done. The public interest can be served by 'private' (commercial) and non-profit organizations as well as by 'public' (state) agencies. 'Public' (state-based) organizations (such as state sector unions) may have their own specific concerns that have little to do with the public interest, or may run directly counter to it. On the other hand, businesses and not-for-profit groups may fulfil tasks relevant to the public interest more effectively than can state actors. Because an agency operates outside the sphere of the state, it does not follow that its concerns are intrinsically selfish, still less that the consequences of its activities necessarily are. Moreover 'state', 'commercial' and 'non-profit' organizations each cover a variety of different forms of organization, which can collaborate with others in a range of ways. All can contribute to the public interest – or frustrate it.

Such a perspective does not imply that decisions about how best to sustain and develop public institutions are a wholly pragmatic matter. New Labour has done itself damage by arguing that 'what counts is what works', which suggests that no ideological factors are involved. Such factors are and should be involved. A given course of action is justified if it demonstrably serves the public interest more effectively than other options. The criteria are in practice not always easy to identify and may quite often be subtle. In deciding whether a given area of activity should be privatized or not, for instance, we have to bear in mind social and cultural consequences as well as economic ones. Privatizing a local bus system might have consequences for people's feelings of ownership and belonging in the community. Since such public goods are of considerable importance, such concerns must at least be brought into the framework of decision-making.

'Third Way, Phase Two'

Following the various social experiments and experiences of the postwar period, we have a clear understanding of what the basic contours of the *good society* should be like, a model that New Labour should adopt. A good society is not one where the state has a dominant role. It is one where the three main sets of social institutions – the state, the economy, and civil society or civic culture, are in balance. What happens when the state becomes too powerful was all too visible in the Soviet Union and the societies of Eastern Europe. But even the weaker forms of collectivism that existed in the heyday of classical social democracy would be unacceptable to most citizens today. State power must be offset by the other institutional sectors.

The good society requires a competitive market economy, a source not only of economic development but of individual freedom, for markets in principle allow free choices to be made by producers and consumers. But the market has the socially damaging traits already alluded to. Market mechanisms cannot substitute either for political and democratic rights, or for the mechanisms of civil society. Citizenship is not the same as the right to roam the aisles of a supermarket.

A healthy civil society or civic order is the condition both of democratic government and of a market economy – as we can see when it is poorly developed. Yet a social order where the state and markets are too weak – where civil society is too dominant and its divisions uncontained – would be as problematic as one where either is too powerful. In the worst cases such conditions produce open conflict, as in Northern Ireland.

4

What Kind of Society Should Britain Become?

The answer to this question is clear and Labour should have no qualms about articulating it. We should want a society that is more egalitarian than it is today, but which is meritocratic and pluralistic; where the devolution of government is further advanced, but within a unitary nation; which is marked by a deepening environmental consciousness; and where there is a restoration of the public sphere and public power.

Meritocracy and equality

Difficult trade-offs – as discussed already – surround the issue of economic inequality. There are even possible trade-offs to be faced in the relation between equality and the revival of public institutions. Thus persuading talented people to choose a career in public service, and providing the incentives that will drive improvements in social status and efficiency, are likely to mean increasing the level of rewards available, thus expanding income differentials.

The existence of such trade-offs is one reason, although not the only one, why a meritocratic approach to inequality is inevitable. They limit what can be achieved. But a meritocratic order, or one that goes some way towards it, should be valued for its own sake. Fluidity is morally as well as economically desirable, since talented individuals have the chance to live up to their potential.

It is important for the centre-left to develop a dynamic, life-chances approach to inequality – one that reconciles equality with cultural and lifestyle diversity. The clashes between freedom and equality to which classical liberals have always pointed are real, and cannot be thought away. Yet equality is also a medium of freedom, since formal freedoms cannot be actualized without resources. Economist Amartya Sen's concept of 'social capability' provides the best way for social democrats to think about these issues.[25] Equality and inequality don't just refer to income, or to the availability of material goods – the disadvantaged need to be able to make effective use of them. Policies concerned with promoting equality should be focused upon developing people's capacities to pursue their well-being. This approach provides a solid philosophical grounding for meritocratic policies, and one that dovetails well with the emphasis of the new social democracy upon investing in education and skills.

It also shows why countering social exclusion is so essential. What matters about poverty isn't economic deprivation as such, but the consequences of such deprivation for individuals' autonomy. Someone whose life is blighted by unwanted poverty is in a different position from that of a person who chooses to live frugally. The crucial thing is precisely the element of autonomy or choice.

A stress upon equality as equality of opportunity presumes redistribution, for two main reasons. One is that wealth and income must be redistributed across the generations. Otherwise, increased inequality of opportunity in one generation may produce inequality of opportunity in the next, since those who do well will look to transfer their advantages to their children. The other is that there has to be social protection for those whose opportunities to progress

39

are limited, or who are left behind when others do well. They should not be denied the chance to lead fulfilling lives. We can make a principle of this observation: no meritocracy without social protection.

Most mobility, by definition, is bound to be short-range mobility, as sociologists call it – movement between occupations fairly close to one another in income and social status. Yet avenues of mobility must also be opened up to allow movement from bottom to top, the true mark of a meritocratic society. New Labour has not exhausted the possibilities that exist to pursue such a goal, mainly because it has been too wary of tackling inequalities at the top. Just as in the case of dealing with poverty, no single policy will be sufficient. We have to look for a package of measures, always remembering they must fall within the bounds of what is electorally feasible.

Should Labour have contemplated raising the top level of income tax for the highest category of earners, which remains at 40 per cent – as proposed among others by the Fabian Commission on Taxation and Citizenship? Why not push up the top rate to 50 per cent for those earning over £100,000 a year? The arguments pro and con are more finely balanced than might be imagined, and on the whole the decision to rule out such an increase was the right one.

If the top rate were raised in this way, it would generate an additional £3 billion for the Treasury, supposing there were no increase in tax avoidance and evasion – not a great deal in the scheme of things, although it would have a small levelling effect. But in fact there almost certainly would be more avoidance and evasion. Clinton was elected in the US in 1992 on a platform that included tax rises for the more affluent. This change did happen. The top rate of federal taxation was raised from 31 per cent to 39.6 per cent. However, only half the revenue the government anticipated it would acquire was brought in. Nearly 50 per cent of all the income tax paid already in the UK is contributed by the top 10 per cent of income earners. The top 1 per cent pay 20 per cent of all that is paid. Despite the reductions in higher tax rates that have happened since 1978–9, these shares have risen markedly over the period since.

Surveys show there is not a great deal of public support for an increase in the top rate of tax, which is widely seen as penalizing success. In addition, there are bound to be some disincentive effects. Finally, and perhaps most significantly, evidence from a diversity of countries shows that in countering inequality what happens at the delivery end is most crucial. What is important is to generate a high tax take and spend the money on effective social programmes.

In seeking to make more of a dent in inequalities at the top, New Labour should switch its attentions elsewhere. One such direction is corporate remuneration and corporate responsibility more generally. There is a great deal of public resentment against fat cat salaries in business – but little adverse feeling against sports stars, whose pay is sometimes higher, because sports people achieve their salaries in open competition, in which the stars are visibly and demonstrably the best in their field. The same cannot necessarily be said of corporate executives, whose personal enrichment often involves the use of power and privilege without any direct relation to performance.

Labour's one main intervention in this area, the windfall tax, did it no great harm, either in the eyes of the electorate or in the City. The same might be true if measures were found that would ensure that boardroom pay was more closely linked to company performance. Recent examples of company bosses who received big payouts in the wake of the decline, or even complete collapse, of their firms are scandalous and seen to be so by the wider public. Moral suasion has little or no purchase in such circumstances. Further statutory intervention should be (and, as of late 2001, is being) looked at, such as the possibility of extending the rights of shareholders to vote on corporate pay, and rescinding clauses in contracts that permit a pay-off where there is failure.

Some other major sources of inequality in society have barely been touched at all. An example is the fee-paying schools, an obsession of Old Labour, but one that has now apparently slipped out of political consciousness. Yet the inequalities associated with them remain plain to see. Labour's declared policy is to bring standards in the state system up to those of the private schools. It is a laudable and necessary aim. The state system must improve and is improving. The introduction of greater diversity and more specialist schools will help. But the private schools can respond by further upgrading their performance and thereby keeping ahead. Private schools cannot be abolished. Such a proposal would not only be a non-starter politically, it would run counter to European human rights legislation. Altering their charitable status can be looked at, but it might be both politically problematic and even iniquitous. Parents who pay school fees, after all, also pay taxes.

What could be done, however, is to open up access to the private schools. The Sutton Trust has suggested one possible approach to this issue.[26] If sufficient resources were made available, admission to private schools could be on a needs-blind basis. Entry would be purely on merit, regardless of ability to pay. Anyone who gained admission would be guaranteed a place, with funding provided for the less well-off. A pilot scheme in a school in Liverpool has proved successful, with students from poorer, and ethnically mixed, backgrounds being much more strongly represented than they were before. The Trust suggests a larger exploratory scheme, involving schools joining up on a voluntary basis. If this venture is effective, with a mixture of government and private funding it could be expanded much more widely. A needs-blind admission approach would be demonstrably different from the old assisted places one. It was right to abolish that scheme, because it was too partial and much abused. But as a consequence the division between state and private schooling looms larger than ever.

Pluralism and regionalism

Meritocracy and pluralism are connected. A pluralistic society is one in which a diversity of groups and cultures coexist, and where they all have a chance to prosper. The UK has become a multicultural society, incorporating a variety of different ethnic and religious groups. Pluralism, however, also means recognizing national, regional and local diversity, and hence connects with Labour's programme for devolution and the revival of local government.

The patchwork nature of Labour's programme of decentralization reflects the seeming reluctance with which it was embraced. Following the 1997 election, Labour moved fast to honour the election pledges that had been made, but was notoriously reluctant to accept what they entailed – the movement of power downwards and away from Whitehall. Having granted devolved powers, the central government was apparently unprepared for the assertions of autonomy that ensued. An attempt to insert an 'acceptable' leader in Wales failed, as it did in London.

The 1997 manifesto contained a commitment to lay the groundwork for a new layer of regional government in England. Eight Regional Development Agencies (RDAs) were set up early in 1999. There is provision for regional chambers, but only on a voluntary, non-statutory basis. The 1997 manifesto had in fact proposed that the English regions would be able to hold referenda to decide whether they wanted elected assemblies.

Since 1997 the government has also issued a series of papers on the restructuring of local government, covering among other areas the issue of elected mayors. The local state needs reform just as much as the national state, and of course the two processes have to be connected. The Local Government Act, passed in 2000, embodied various policies for improving the efficiency, transparency and accountability of local administration. Councils are to have new constitutions and separate executives regardless of whether or not a directly elected mayor is chosen. Directly elected mayors exist in a number of EU countries and in the US, but they are a new departure for the UK. As the draft Local Government Bill put it, they introduce 'an entirely new form of democratic mandate into our system of local government' and this is why a referendum is necessary before a city adopts such a system.[27] Old habits die hard, however. Most of the discussion and legislative documents published by the government on regional and local autonomy are still top-down in orientation, specifying what councils and other agencies of local government may or may not do.

There is strong evidence of the need to stimulate local and regional democracy in Britain. A recent study of electoral turnout in European countries in local elections, for example, showed Britain at the very bottom of the table. Turnout in Denmark, Germany and France was 80 per cent, 72 per cent and 68 per cent respectively. In Britain it was 40 per cent. Just over a third of electors voted in London, and there were some wards in England with turnouts of just over 10 per cent.[28]

Among those who are lukewarm towards devolution in England, much has been made of the narrowness of the Welsh vote in favour of an assembly. With one or two exceptions, such as the North East, they point out there is little popular pressure to develop English regionalism. However, the constitutional changes that have already been enacted in Scotland and Wales will almost certainly stimulate greater regional consciousness elsewhere. Moreover, the arguments in favour of devolution in England are compelling. It can be an instrument of economic regeneration and democratization. Without it, other political influences might move in: 'By giving little encouragement to the forces in favour of democratic regionalism, and palming off the regions with development agencies answerable only to ministers in London, a space is left open for the Little Englanders to occupy.'[29]

A more worked-out programme of English regional development is required, preferably with a timetable attached. Devolution is not a panacea, and some of the difficulties involved have to be considered in advance as well as the benefits spelled out. Various reports produced by Labour, including some dating from the early 1990s, have broached the issues. The document *A Choice for England* analysed how the Conservatives had produced an 'invisible and unaccountable' regional state in England with the introduction of numerous quangos. Regional government, the report argued, will not produce another layer of bureaucracy, because there is already one in place – bureaucracy should be supplanted by increased democracy.

The differing experience of devolution in Scotland, Wales and London creates a strong case that, if regional government in England were to be established, it should be given serious powers which should include legislative and tax-raising capacities. But the devil lies in the detail, and many questions remain. Exactly what will the relationship be between assemblies and local councils? How much influence should regional assemblies have over national government? What relationship will there be between the powers of elected mayors and those of regional assemblies? Difficult though these and other questions may be to answer, they will not go away. Far better to confront them openly than to muddle along in a constitutional limbo. Moreover, other countries that have more devolved systems of government provide examples from which we can learn.

There are signs that the government is ready to take a stronger and more positive line on English regionalism, and other forms of local autonomy in the UK, with a new White Paper to be published soon. At the moment loose ends are dangling almost everywhere, and major difficulties of the kind just noted remain. The complete regional remake that took place in Spain after the death of Franco would be impossible to achieve in England, or in the UK more generally. Yet the Spanish experience does give some clues as to what can be achieved through thoroughgoing devolution. The creation of the autonomous communities in Spain has played a part in the impressive economic progress the country has made over past decades. Some have more autonomy than others, but although this causes problems and conflicts, they seem to be manageable. When the autonomous communities were set up, areas like Catalonia already had strongly developed cultural and linguistic identities, grounded in a long history. Others had virtually no established regional identity at all. What is interesting is that, since they were given autonomy, such areas have quickly acquired firm identities, with which many of the population have come to identify.

Greater regional and local autonomy means the freedom to do things differently, to have different priorities from central government. It is not only very distinct from government from Whitehall, it is something for which British political culture as a whole is not well prepared. Most of the public still look first of all to national government as the means of protecting their interests. However, these attitudes are likely to change if significant further devolution is achieved.

A recent survey carried out in Spain investigated people's views of the autonomous communities. The results showed only 16 per cent in favour of returning to the national structure that existed before devolution; 44 per cent were in favour of the system of autonomous communities as it now exists; 21 per cent supported the view that the autonomous communities should have more power than they do now; 8 per cent were in favour of complete independence for them. The remainder held no specific views on the issues.[30]

Devolution to the nations and regions should be seen as a means of keeping the state intact, not of dismembering it. Labour is committed to keeping Britain as a unitary country, and this goal can be justified in broad-ranging ideological terms. We should seek to build or sustain what I have elsewhere called a 'cosmopolitan nation' in the UK, resisting the extremes of identity politics.[31] A cosmopolitan nation is one able to tolerate, and to some extent integrate, different cultural and regional identities. Keeping Scotland, Wales and, for the foreseeable future, Northern Ireland within the UK is more than a matter of political expediency or inertia. It corresponds to the need to limit the endless fragmentation of nations along the lines of ethnicity which identity politics produces. The extremes to which such a process can lead can readily be seen in ex-Yugoslavia, where a patchwork of ethnically separate states or statelets now exist, quite often where the groups involved had lived harmoniously alongside one another before.

Countries can divide without any such conflicts at all. The break-up of Czechoslovakia, for instance, happened in a peaceful way. The same would be true if Scotland declared its independence from the UK, if Belgium split in two, Catalonia broke away from Spain, or even if the north of Italy seceded from the rest. But none of these is a desirable outcome. Nations need to be able to reconcile linguistic, ethnic and cultural diversity within their own borders if they are also to be able to do so outside.

Environmental modernization

Ten years before New Labour came to power, Margaret Thatcher declared her conversion to the environmental cause. 'We do not have a freehold on the earth,' she said, 'only a full repairing lease.' However, her declaration was not translated into effective policy changes. Compared to the leading continental countries, the UK in the early 1990s had a poor record in many fields of environmental concern. Britain was widely condemned as the 'dirty man of Europe', because of not living up to its environmental commitments. A survey carried out in 1993 reported that 58 per cent of Britain's trees were severely or moderately blighted by acid rain – the worst record of thirty-four countries in west and central Europe, including several former communist states. Between 1990 and 1995, air quality in Britain went down by 35 per cent, according to an official report of the Department of the Environment. The environmental costs of air pollution were estimated at £15 billion per year in 1996. Such pollution hastened the deaths of some 25,000 vulnerable people annually.

The UK continued to dump large amounts of untreated sewage into the North Sea after other countries had stopped doing so. Although a programme was set up to improve polluted beaches, at the time at which Labour came into power in 1997 fifty-one beaches in the UK were still below the EU prescribed level. A high proportion of rivers and lakes also failed to meet EU standards. A Royal Commission in 1992 found that 400 towns had drinking water that contained toxic materials.

Britain launched BSE into the world. At first apparently confined to the UK, BSE has now spread to other European countries, and may become a global problem. When fears were first raised that eating infected beef could affect humans, the Tory government resolutely denied the possibility. The link was recognized as proven in September 1997, as a result of the increasing weight of scientific evidence. Some 1.5 million cows infected with BSE probably passed into the food chain before that date. So far some seventy lives have been lost to CJD, the related human disease. It is impossible to say whether or not many other people, perhaps thousands, have been infected, since the incubation period for the disease is unknown.

Labour came into office determined to improve upon this record. The departments of Transport and Environment were merged soon after Labour took office in 1997, with the aim of developing a cohesive strategy of sustainable development. (Following the 2001 election, they were broken up again, with environmental responsibilities transferred to a new Department of Environment, Food and Rural Affairs.) An audit committee was set up to monitor environmental progress across the whole range of government departments. A White Paper on integrated transport, with a strong environmental slant, was published in 1998. All local councils, plus RDAs, were asked to prepare five-year transport plans, covering the lowering of pollution, reduction of traffic and improvement in public transport. Councils were given powers to raise revenue from road congestion and workplace parking charges, the money raised going towards environmental improvement.

Environmental issues were also addressed in fiscal reforms. Landfill tax was increased. Measures were taken to encourage building insulation. Car licence charges were reduced for vehicles with smaller engines and raised for those with engines having larger cubic capacity. An energy tax designed to help to meet climate control objectives was put on the statute book and has come into operation. New Labour agreed to sign up to a range of international agreements on ecological questions, especially the key agreements on climate change. According to the Kyoto Protocol of December 1997, the industrial countries will reduce their emissions of greenhouse gases by an average of 5.2 per cent below 1990 levels over a specified period. The UK has agreed to lower its emissions by 12.5 per cent.

In October 2000, Tony Blair delivered his most comprehensive speech on ecological issues thus far, followed by a further speech in March 2001. He appeared to accept that the efforts made by the government at that point had been inadequate to the scale of environmental problems. With many other questions to concentrate on in its first years, as he put it, 'environmental issues slid back down the political agenda.' Such issues, he continued, must be brought more to the forefront, as the 1997 manifesto originally promised, since 'the environmental challenge continues to grow more urgent.' Progress has been made since then, but there remains a great deal to do.

The strategies needed to cope with ecological problems are actually consistent with the main emphases of the new social democracy. State intervention and regulation are needed at all levels, including using market-based instruments to control risks and develop relevant technologies. The costs of such measures are often less than might be thought, because market pressures generate many cost-reducing responses to policy innovations. The use of market instruments – taxes, tax incentives, the trading of rights, certain forms of futures trading and so forth – in environmental policy can and should be comprehensive.

It is important to recognize that, the relatively poor record of the UK notwithstanding, advances have been made in the industrial countries, including the UK, over the past few years – by a mix of governmental intervention and market-driven influences. Across the EU as a whole the recycling of waste is far more developed than even ten years ago, air quality is higher, and the pollution of rivers and the shoreline has been reduced.

There is an enormous amount still to achieve, at national, regional and international levels, and political problems to be faced in mobilizing the necessary solutions. Agreement was reached in Bonn in late 2001 on implementing the Kyoto proposals – but the US remained outside. It is generally agreed that more far-reaching measures are needed to control global warming. The policies of national governments can make a big difference. The environmental case for elevating energy taxes still higher in the UK, for example, is strong – and has few implications for either job creation or growth rates.[32]

Better and more determined political leadership on environmental issues will be required from New Labour than was evident in its first term. There are some policy orientations that can help. Wherever possible, consumption taxes should be structured around incentives – tax breaks for exemplary behaviour – rather than as punitive regulation. A clear link should be made between energy taxes and potential or real reductions in income and payroll taxes, as Labour has done with the climate change levy. The ecological benefits of energy taxes need to be clearly spelled out. New Labour has done only a little better than the Tories on these issues, at least until the recent policy innovations. Fuel taxes were raised by the Conservatives under Mrs Thatcher to pay for the cuts in top-rate income tax that she introduced. But this connection was never made public, or put in a positive way. Nor was it made so when New Labour first continued the fuel escalator (later dropped), which was mainly treated as a means of raising revenue rather than publicly defended as an environmental policy.

An emphasis upon ecological modernization is an essential part of the environmental agenda and should be integrated within New Labour's wider modernization programme. Ecological modernization refers to the quest to combine higher levels of economic development with lower levels of environmental impact. It is more or less fully compatible with the shift in the macro economy towards knowledge-based and service industries, but only if technological change is linked to a strategic agenda. 'Public intervention', as Albert Weale puts it, 'is an essential part of ensuring a progressive relationship between industry and environment . . . implicit is a positive role for public authority in raising the standards of environmental regulation, as a means of providing a spur to industrial innovation.'[33] Where older-type industries still prevail, a strategy of ecological modernization has even more importance, since there is often no 'natural convergence' between trends of development and environmental objectives.

Those countries that have made most progress in implementing ecological modernization policies, such as the Netherlands, Germany, Norway, Sweden and Japan, have given them a strong local and regional orientation. Here again we come up against the partial character of New Labour's approach to devolution. The RDAs are supposed to help implement environmentally progressive policies, and the language of environmental modernization sometimes appears in official accounts of regional policy in the UK. Labour has revived strategic planning, creating new Regional Economic Strategies. The central theme for regional strategic plans is sustainability. RDAs are supposed to work with Regional Local Government Associations, the Government Office for the Regions and Regional Chambers. But government and business appear as the proactive elements, while consumers are seen as largely passive. There is no real framework for direct democratic involvement and accountability. Current policy 'relies upon a narrow technocratic and instrumental approach rather than being integrative and communicative. This approach will not lead to the type of embedded cultural transformations that will sustain factors such as environmental improvements, reduced consumption and greater equity.'[34]

A new approach to ecological issues must be based on the recognition that these questions are absolutely central to the political agenda, and this recognition must be backed with policy. The concept of social security in the past has been restricted to the risks covered by orthodox welfare institutions – such as job loss, illness or disablement. We have to extend it to embrace environmental risks, given that they can impinge so directly upon people's everyday lives. The risks associated with food provide a good example. Britain is by no means the only country to have faced food scares, real and imagined, in recent years. Citizens have a right to security in their consumption of food just as they do in other contexts of their activities – and government has an obligation to help meet this need. To have confidence in what we eat demands regulatory mechanisms. The UK has not had as effective an agency as the Food and Drug Administration in the United States, but there is no reason why the standards set by the FDA should not be rivalled, or surpassed, here. Environmental risks do not stop at the borders of the nation-state, and a toughening of international standards in food production and processing is necessary and urgent. Environmental risks, the risks associated with science and technology, financial and economic risk, overlap with one another as never before. Tackling them must be brought within the mainstream political framework, not relegated to when specific crises occur.

Discussion of the future of public institutions seems like a traditional 'red' issue, distinct from the newer green anxieties and problems. Environmental strategies, however, are vital to public concerns. Environmental innovation, as part of the process of ecological modernization, is a public good, and should be supported by state investment as well as by the sophisticated use of regulation and tax instruments to promote technological advance.

5

The Revival of Public Services

General issues

Few areas are as affected by dogma and misunderstandings as controversies about the future of public services. Each of the four prejudices I noted at the beginning reigns in full. It is a notorious political minefield, where a whole range of special interests are in play, and where those interests are liable to legitimate themselves by claiming to represent the public good.

Insularity in particular breeds myths about public institutions. There is no doubt that some public services in Britain are markedly inferior to best practice examples from countries elsewhere. But the differences can be exaggerated. Take the railways. It is often said that France has a far more efficient and safe railway system than the UK, because so much taxpayers' money has been invested in it – just look at the wonderful TGVs. They are indeed wonderful, but the rest of the system lags some way behind. The proportion of people travelling by train and the amount of freight carried in France were both dropping in the 1990s. There were public scandals and kick-backs involved in the development of the TGV project, which suffered from huge cost overruns.[35] In 2001 the French railways were running at a loss of 1.7 billion euros a year. The true figure was much higher, because there was a government subsidy of 1.6 billion euros annually. The long-term debt incurred by the system is 22.8 billion euros; 2.4 billion euros are paid out per year simply to cover interest charges on this debt.

A comparative outlook is vital when considering the relation between state and private involvement in the provision of public services. Labour's promise to increase state spending on the NHS to the European average, for instance, has to be seen in context. State spending on health care in the UK, as a proportion of GDP, does lag behind that of some other EU countries, but not by much. Thus, as of 2000, state expenditure on the health service amounted to 5.7 per cent of GDP, compared to 5.5 per cent in Italy, 5.8 per cent in Austria, 6 per cent in the Netherlands and around 7 per cent in France and Germany. The EU average was just over 6 per cent. Most EU countries pay out considerably more than Britain on health care, but this is primarily because of the much higher involvement of private resources, especially in the shape of discretionary charges. In Germany, more than half of all hospitals are run by independent providers, contracting out services to the state or insurers. Private (non-state) involvement is 31 per cent in Italy, 24 per cent in France, 21 per cent in Finland – and only 15 per cent in the UK.

Let me at this juncture recall one or two points made earlier and add to them. The condition of Britain's public services does not just reflect lower taxation levels than most other EU countries, but also organizational and economic problems from which the country has suffered. In discussing public sector reform we must again not forget the need to integrate social and economic policy. 'Public' versus 'private' is not a straightforward distinction. There are many ways of delivering public services and many different combinations of state and non-state agencies. Non-state agencies include not-for-profit trusts, third sector and voluntary organizations. We must be careful not to overgeneralize from single examples to whole sectors of provision. Those who want a large role for the state have their favourite stories of how private projects, or public–private partnerships, have gone wrong, led to corruption, profiteering and so forth. People who have greater faith in markets have their own choice examples of state incompetence, cost overruns and bureaucratic dithering. Nothing is gained by the ritual name-calling that results from such misapplied comparisons.

It is important to point out that there are large areas of the state sector in which there is already a great deal of private and other non-state involvement. Residential and nursing home provision, for instance, used to be almost completely funded and managed by local authorities and the NHS; 75 per cent is still paid for by taxpayers' money, but the private sector provides 80 per cent of the services. Under the Tories 1.75 million council houses were sold to their occupiers. But since the late 1980s a further half a million homes have been transferred to housing associations and local housing companies – a process that is still continuing. These groups still often receive state funding, but make use of private capital and contractors in most of what they do.[36]

Privatization versus state control

As with other areas of its programme, many of the policies New Labour developed towards public services in its first term are correct and should be persisted with – including some that have proved highly controversial. Thus it is essential to couple increasing investment in public services to reform. Some of the inadequacies of Britain's public services are more to do with inertia, poor management, overmanning and bureaucratic sloth than lack of resources. Given the rapid pace of innovation in business, and the advance of technology, a great deal of change is necessary for the state sector to catch up.

The Revival of Public Services

Labour has faced a barrage of criticism from leftist circles for its determination to bring public–private partnerships into the delivery of public services. Yet whatever the rights and wrongs of specific PPP projects – such as the hot potato of the London Underground – in a general way it is right to do so. PPPs can take a variety of forms, and do so in different countries. PPPs have been set up in so many societies around the world that some have spoken of them as the 'new global paradigm' in public administration.[37] All EU states are using them, some from a long while back. The European Commission has devised a legal framework for the development of partnerships – they now account for 11 per cent of the EU's gross domestic product, and this proportion is rising. In Eastern Europe, PPPs are seen as a means of restructuring public services to meet public needs, but also as a way of developing a civil society in the wake of communism.

The backdrop to the increasing prominence of PPPs is dissatisfaction both with state sector provision of public services and with privatization. Privatization was thought of by the Thatcherites as a radical solution to the well-established problems and limitations of the state. This view was to some degree correct. Governments all over the world have embarked on privatization programmes. The privatization of state-owned or state-controlled industries has often been successful. In some areas, when combined with competitive markets, and where the privatizing process has been handled competently and fairly, the results have been positive and sometimes even spectacular. Privatization in these circumstances can create top-class companies, reduce costs and improve services to consumers. Who in Britain would want to go back to when it took weeks to get a new telephone line?

Yet overall the results of privatization have been mixed. The reasons are partly generic. Thus privatization becomes problematic wherever it is difficult to introduce effective market-based competition and incentives. However, privatization is not cut of the whole cloth. There have been good and there have been poor privatizations, and there are lessons to be learned from mistakes that have been made.

The Treasury's own report on PPPs, *Public Private Partnerships*, lays out succinctly why some privatizations in the UK were much less successful than they might have been. Businesses were sometimes sold for much less than their true value. Assets were disposed of too quickly and cheaply. The valuations did not take into account the degree to which commercial pressures and incentives in the private sector would improve performance. Not enough was done to dissolve unnecessary elements of monopoly that remained in place. Regulation was often too lax, and proved an inadequate substitute for the market. And, as the Treasury document puts it drily, senior management was 'often enriched beyond any reasonable requirements for incentives to achieve commercial success and with insufficient direct link to performance'.[38]

The windfall tax was introduced by the Labour government in recognition of the fact that the utilities had been sold off too cheaply. The utilities provide a prime example where state sector monopolies were transferred to commercial companies with significant monopoly characteristics remaining intact. These considerations do not destroy the case for privatization. They do show how important it is fully to debate and scrutinize privatizations before they are undertaken. Unless it is clear that questions of monopoly and regulation can be dealt with, the privatization of major industries should probably always be partial in the first instance. Mistakes can be corrected before they become too serious. Once it has taken place, the privatization of a large industrial sector is difficult to reverse, because of the costs and the resistances involved. In the wake of the collapse of Railtrack, the government has proposed a solution short of full renationalization. Yet the decision to put

Railtrack into administration has provoked a bitter City and shareholder backlash. The issue of shareholder compensation not only affects those who were profiteering from a firm they believed would always be bailed out by government. Many small shareholders, some of them Railtrack employees, put their savings into the company.

The privatization of British Rail was politically motivated, hasty, ham-fisted and ill thought through. But privatization is not the main cause of the troubles of the UK's rail system. The inadequacies of the railways reflect a combination of underinvestment and poor management that goes back many decades. The revenues of Railtrack were determined from day one of its existence by a formula set up by the regulator. But there was no inventory of the condition of the track and signals. No one knew then how much it would cost to refurbish the system. Only later did it come to light what a mess had been inherited from the days of nationalization.

There are few if any other railway systems in the world that are wholly privatized, but many countries are experimenting with letting the private sector in. The current government in Japan is considering fully privatizing three formerly state-run national railway companies by the middle of 2002. The companies have been substantially privatized for some while. At the moment the government holds a 12.5 per cent stake in one, 31.5 per cent in another and 39.7 per cent in a third. The privatizing of the Japanese railways has not been unproblematic, but the rail system there continues to have high standards of efficiency and safety.

In the changing circumstances of today, some are talking about the possibility of a revival of statism and of Keynesianism. We are seeing, they say, a return to state intervention and pump-priming investment. The US government, for instance, a Republican administration at that, is providing financial assistance to beleaguered airlines. The Swiss and the Belgians have done something similar (although Sabena has now gone out of business), while the British government may be forced to step in to save British Airways, should it fall further into difficulties. At the same time we are witnessing a retreat from privatization, as the example of Railtrack proves. Rather than more privatization, it is claimed, we should be thinking of returning some basic services to state ownership and control.

These arguments, however, are incorrect. The Railtrack episode does indeed teach us something about the limits of privatization. But it tells us just as much about the failings of nationalization. British Rail was starved of cash and inefficiently managed for years before privatization came on the scene. It may be rational for governments to give temporary support for airlines, because the disappearance of a national carrier might have wider economic effects on a country – it could, for instance, affect the tourist industry if some routes are no longer flown. But few are likely to contemplate renationalizing companies, given the managerial problems and costs to the taxpayer that have marked state airlines in the past. Governments may need to intervene in some other circumstances, such as where an industrial closure has widespread social effects, or to ease adjustment to technological change. Such situations will be more common when the external economic environment is poor than when it is benign. But there will be no general return to statism, because the conditions in which it flourished no longer pertain, and because its weaknesses have become so apparent.

The private finance initiative

Private–public partnerships under Labour are not supposed to supplant privatization or traditional state sector management, but to add a new dimension – one that, in best practice cases, can draw upon the capabilities offered by the state and the private sector, and integrate them. PPPs, it is said, 'enable the Government to tap into the disciplines, incentives, skills and expertise which private sector firms have developed in the course of their normal everyday business and so release the full potential of the people, knowledge and assets in the public sector'.[39]

In the UK the private finance initiative has thus far been the main type of public–private partnership. In PFI, private companies fund, construct and own assets, while the state makes a long-term commitment to purchase the services thus provided. In 2000–1 PFI deals accounted for nearly a fifth of publicly sponsored capital spending. Six new hospitals have been constructed using PFI schemes since 1997, and a further twenty-one are under way. All four new prisons built since 1997 have been built under PFI agreements. PFI contracts are in place to upgrade the plant of no fewer than 450 schools. The most significant, area, however, is transport, which accounts for well over 70 per cent of all current PFI projects.

PFI offers advantages in some contexts over orthodox state sector ventures. Once a PFI contract has been signed, it is more difficult for government to interfere, or renege on the commitment at a later date. In principle, this feature makes possible long-term investment planning. Government departments previously were often unable to make firm commitments in the long term, since their budgets were never known for more than a short while ahead. Moreover, firms working in the commercial sector are likely on average to be better managed than state agencies – not merely because they are commercial, but because they have been exposed to competition. In a market, unlike in the sphere of the state, poorly managed companies will be driven out of business.

A Danish study of forty-one public investments in transport showed that in more than 75 per cent of them construction costs, when adjusted for inflation, exceeded the projections by at least 10 per cent, and in half the cases exceeded them by 50 per cent.[40] The researchers concluded that this phenomenon is a systematic one in state-provided services. In decision-making and the execution of projects, public officials are swayed by optimistic forecasts – they give in all the more easily because they know they will not be penalized for mistakes. The private sector is not immune from such influences, but errors are less common because economic penalties follow.

In contrast to conventional state sector projects, in PFI agreements up-front state investment is not required. Projects can hence in principle be undertaken without increasing the public sector borrowing requirement (PSBR). However, just as in orthodox public sector projects, there is a commitment to fund the debt, in the form of a service contract. PFI is no more than a handy – and spurious – accounting device if it does not provide a significant transfer of risk. The key question in evaluating PFI is whether or not risk is taken over sufficiently by the private sector. If it is not, then PFI projects should in any case really count against the PSBR.

The critics of PFI are vociferous in claiming that it is an expensive means of funding public projects, since the government can borrow money more cheaply by going directly to the capital markets. However, the comparison made here is false. The reason is that PFI builds in the cost of risk, while the conventional method masks it.[41] A preference for orthodox borrowing is sensible for any individual agency undertaking a project, but risk is then transferred to the rest of the public sector without being costed. As compared to PFI, the public sector now has one more diffuse risk than it had before. There is a clear rationale for PFI in those contexts where it is relatively easy to write contracts that cover all major contingencies – as is usually the case, for example, with road-building.

As in other sectors, there are good and bad PFI projects. Some contractors, state and private, will do a better job than others. Yet despite the intensity of the criticisms made by opponents, there seems no reason to doubt that the majority of existing PFI projects will be effective. The point of comparison is not an ideal state of affairs, but what could have been achieved had a conventional state sector approach been used instead – the so-called 'public sector comparator'.

The main problem is not PFI as such, but the fact that it has been to date so much the dominant type of partnership. Many different forms of partnership exist in other countries, in which the 'private' or non-state element is much more prominent than in the UK – and where the level of public service delivered is higher than here also. We need to explore these more thoroughly in this country than has been achieved so far.

The future of public provision

More extensive partnerships between state and non-state groups in key public services in general are inevitable if such services really are to be brought up to a better standard. New Labour has not done a good job of explaining why, or of convincing the electorate that such an approach will not undermine the public service ethic. There are several ways of so doing. One is to drive home the message that the public realm is not to be equated with the state, and that therefore partnership is not the same as privatization. Most citizens surely understand the point well, but Old Labour was so closely associated with the state that a special effort needs to be made to stress it. Taking on sectional interests, including where necessary public sector unions, helps. But the case needs to be laid out much more positively.

The public interest is not well served wherever there is less competition, tight financial control, innovation and effective autonomy in decision-making in an existing service than alternative arrangements can offer. A great deal of evidence from other industrial countries is available to help show what alternatives there are for orthodox state bureaucracies in public service delivery.

Those who oppose further non-state involvement in public services often argue that the public service ethos becomes corroded where state organizations combine with others. Yet this argument is at most only partly valid, and there is again a certain memory loss coming into play here. A commitment to serve the community underlies the dedication many public service employees have towards their work. But state sector organizations are not the only ones in which there is a spirit of service. And in the past there was often a strong downside. State agencies were sometimes marked by attitudes of indifference to the needs of citizens, secrecy and unaccountability that would be unthinkable now. As Martin Summers has pointed out, speaking of local government:

> one of the most valuable benefits of opening up what have traditionally been local government domains to outside organisations – whether they be commercial organisations, quangos, charities, NHS trusts or housing associations – is that there has been the opportunity to see how different means of decision-making perform; thus presenting alternatives to the traditional monolithic, hierarchical and departmentalised local authority model.[42]

There are other gains that partnership or collaboration can generate. Contact with public organizations can produce significant changes in the outlook and behaviour of private firms too. When involved with public projects, such firms are called upon to act differently from how they might do in the open marketplace – in respect, for instance, of disclosure of information, integrity and accountability.[43] Labour's approach obscures these possibilities, because the private sector has been turned to mainly when state agencies are seen to fail, and because it has concentrated mainly on drawing in commercial firms when it has done so – as with failing schools. The messages conveyed here are wrong. They suggest that private involvement is important only when state institutions are unable to cope, and then only around the margins. They also imply that the only choice is between state organizations and commercial ones. But a variety of non-state agencies, including mutuals, social enterprises, not-for-profit trusts and public benefit corporations, can and should be brought into the delivery of public services.[44]

In all industrial countries over the past thirty years the status and remuneration of workers in the public services have suffered compared to many working in the private marketplace. A generation ago a career in the civil service, health care or teaching was widely seen as attractive. It offered social prestige, reasonable levels of pay and a high degree of job security. These attractions have declined relative to the advantages offered by the private sector.

This trend can and should be challenged, without seeking to return to social conditions of the past that no longer apply today. The difficulty is that this has to go along with reform and the need to persuade workers to break away from comfortable or ingrained habits and bureaucratic practices. The approach adopted by Labour is one that has been called 'challenge and support'. Challenge means the use of criticism, assessment and incentives to encourage change; support means ensuring that the system is well funded and that staff get proper recognition for their work. The early postwar period, it might be said, leaned towards support with little challenge. When Thatcherism took hold, this relationship swung radically the other way. There was a period of much challenge and little support – producing declining morale in the public services. The question now is to find a better relationship between the two. New Labour in its first term did not really create that better relationship – there was too much reliance on the methods and outlook introduced by the Thatcher governments. It must move away from this perspective if more staff are to be attracted into the public services and kept there. The NHS plan published in July 2000 envisages recruiting 7,500 more consultants, 2,000 more GPs and no fewer than 20,000 more nurses by 2004. But these ambitions, like similar ones to recruit more teachers into schools, will prove difficult to realize unless support is brought ahead of challenge.

Pay, decent conditions of work, control over work circumstances, status and esteem are what determine how far a given job or type of job will prove attractive. Overall levels of pay for public sector workers can be, and have been, increased since 1997. Even though it doesn't help with the overall quest to reduce inequalities, increased rewards at the top have to be put in place. They form a key part of developing a more aspirational culture in the public services, and in capturing greater social status for them too.

Work conditions and personal autonomy are what count for most. This is one reason why it is so vital to connect reform of public services to decentralization. Labour seems to lack a consistent philosophy of management within public institutions. The most effective forms of management in the business sector are those that have introduced flattened hierarchies, allow for bottom-up decision-making, and cultivate autonomy. These traits could be much further developed in public institutions than has happened so far. They are not compatible with the centralized 'command and control' that remains a persistent feature of some areas of the public services, and aspects of government policy towards them.

In sum, New Labour's approach to the reform of public institutions should be: first, no return to any flirtation with statism – press on with reform of the state and the diversifying of public service provision. Second, the encouragement of partnerships, but with systematic monitoring of performance and outcomes. Third, a continued commitment to improvement in the status and conditions of work of state sector employees, based upon providing good incentives, increased autonomy and continuing managerial reform. Fourth, the forging of a more effective ideological position, which integrates the renewal of public services with a wider commitment to public institutions and the public sphere. This endeavour might be understood as a process of 'publicization', distinct from privatization, but also from the traditional heavy reliance on the state sector.

The government would be wise not to stake too much of its reputation upon its capacity to improve public services. It needs to nurture just as much its capabilities in its stewardship of the economy, the encouragement of technological innovation, the continuing reform of welfare, and the prevention of crime. Much progress can and should be made in upgrading public institutions over the next four years and beyond. But reversing a period of relative decline in public service provision that stretches back over many years demands long-term structural change and investment.

Moreover, in the area of public services as elsewhere endemic difficulties and trade-offs have to be dealt with. All industrial countries are struggling with problems that admit no easy solutions. No matter what incentives are offered, and innovations made, the pay and status of state sector workers will not in the foreseeable future fully rival those in business and commerce. All the ways of providing public services – via the state, not-for-profit organizations, voluntary organizations and the private sector – have their limitations. The same holds for the diverse combinations of them that are possible. The main problems around which there will always be compromises and trade-offs are those of monopoly and the management of risk. The railways are again an example. Railways can be turned over to private operators, but government cannot allow railway companies just to go bust where they provide a key public good. The state continues to shoulder risk, and is expected to do so both by the public and by shareholders. Full market principles do not apply. Real competition, moreover, is impossible in some core parts of the railway business.

However, keeping the railways in state control (or, in the UK, returning them to it) runs up against all the well-established problems that beset state enterprises. The government's current strategy – turning Railtrack into a non-profit trust – has some potential advantages. Yet it has its own ambiguities and problems. If the government is to bail out the company should it get into difficulties, it has shouldered a diffuse risk of substantial proportions. Moreover, the inefficiencies and soft budget controls that marked the nationalized industry might return in a new guise.

6

Internationalism and Globalization

Globalization and anti-globalization

Controversies about globalization are not remote from the domestic agenda, or at least should not be seen as such. Globalization directly affects economic policy, the welfare system, environmental problems, the definition of public goods and much else besides. It is a mistake to see globalization as merely an external force. It is driven in some part by the policies of governments, but also by the day-to-day activities of citizens. Every time someone switches on a computer and links up to the internet he or she is contributing to globalization, not just responding to it. We must bear these considerations in mind when assessing the nature and implications of the anti-globalization movement.

The anti-globalization protestors include a diversity of groups, some with incompatible objectives compared with others. Some are against capitalism *tout court*, although in the nature of the case such groups cannot with any cogency say what they are for. The more moderate protesters, including many of the NGOs involved, have more substantive points to make. They need to be listened to. Globalization, they argue, is essentially driven by the concerns of the West, and is leading to ever greater disparities between the rich and poor nations. Some add that globalization is also responsible for the conflicts and wars that have disfigured global society over the past decade.

New Labour needs a clear and sophisticated position on these questions. Such a position should be consistent with its wider ideological outlook. It should be based on a rejection of neoliberalism or market fundamentalism, and a reassertion of the role of active government in the international arena. It should be pro-globalization, but refuse the identification of globalization with an unqualified advocacy of free trade. It should be multilateral and reformist, aiming to strengthen and reform institutions of global governance. Endeavours to regulate the global economy, such as the efforts of OECD to enforce greater trans-parency in banking practices and control tax havens, should be supported. The rich countries have a responsibility – as well as sound economic and geopolitical reasons – to help poorer countries engage with economic development. International law, especially human rights law, should be strengthened and given stronger purchase.

The UK's involvement in the EU should be understood in this wider context. The EU is pioneering a form of transnational governance, which, if successful, should be of great interest to other regions in the world. The EU today is both a response to and an expression of globalization. Unlike more traditional forms of international organization, like the UN, it is not an assemblage of nation-states. In the EU member nations have voluntarily agreed to cede sovereignty over some aspects of domestic and foreign policy in order to pool their common resources.

Those who are 'against' globalization and those who are 'for' it often radically oversimplify the forces shaping the contemporary world. Several misconceptions about globalization have to be overcome. Globalization should not be identified, as each side in this confrontation tends to, with economic deregulation and the spread of world markets. The core meaning of globalization is increasing interdependence: no matter where we live in the world, we are all affected by events and changes happening many miles away. The development of increasingly integrated world markets has contributed significantly to this phenomenon. But so have other major influences. The most important factors shaping globalization are not those to do with finance and markets, but with communication.[45] The communications revolution, involving a merging of satellite-based electronic communication and computerization, is only some thirty years old. It coincides more or less completely with the origins of globalization in its current form. Instantaneous electronic communication across the world has altered so many aspects of our basic institutions. Without it the economic changes just referred to could not exist. But it has affected almost everything else too, including the activities of the anti-globalization movement itself. The protesters who demonstrated in Seattle, and in many other cities since then, made use of modern systems of communication, such as mobile phones and the internet, to organize their protests. The terrorist attacks on New York and Washington on September 11, 2001 could not have happened without these technologies.

As became obvious after September 11, if it wasn't before, terrorist networks can have a global spread. They represent a different pattern of violence from the past, which for the most part no longer pits state against state.[46] The wars between nations and blocs of nations that caused such havoc in the twentieth century may return to haunt the twenty-first as well. But for the moment it looks more likely that wars will be centred in areas where the state is weak, but where there are international networks and movements involved, sometimes drawing resources from outside governments, but also from drugs, illegal trade in arms and plunder and money laundering.

Confronting these groups will demand more globalization, not less. We can say with some certainty that no significant world problems can be resolved by a retreat from globalization. Coping with the problems of globalization means giving explicit recognition to our increased interdependence and to the cooperative solutions that represent the only feasible means of coping with them.

Inequality and development

The anti-globalization movement blames globalization for the increasing gulf between rich and poor across the world, understanding by 'globalization' the spread of free markets. In fact, it is questionable whether global inequalities are increasing; and globalization, as a variety of research studies show, is not the prime cause of the inequalities that do exist. Many discussions of world inequality have drawn inaccurate conclusions because they are based on comparing the GDP of countries, without taking into account population differences.[47] China is treated as equivalent to a country such as, say, Guatemala, although the former state has a population many times as large. If we look at GDP in relation to population, a different picture emerges from that of ever-increasing inequalities. World inequalities did rise over a period of a century from the middle of the nineteenth century up to the early 1960s. But since that time this trend has been halted. Such a finding conforms to the results of research using a wider range of criteria to measure well-being than just income. In terms of health, nutrition, life expectancy, infant mortality, women's rights and literacy, the developing countries on average are better off than they were thirty years ago and – from a very low starting-point – have closed the gap with the industrial nations.

However, gross comparisons of this sort can easily be misleading, since there are so many differences between countries and regions. It is more sensible to analyse and explain these divergences than to look for blanket explanations or interpretations. In Asia rapid economic development in some countries, including China, has produced spectacular improvements in incomes and living conditions. Korea in 1960 was poorer than Ghana; today it is richer, in average income per head, than Portugal. Inequalities between the successful parts of Asia and the West by definition have declined rather than increased, since Asian average growth rates have been much higher than those of Western countries over the past twenty-five years.

The picture in Latin America, and also particularly in Africa, looks different. Latin America overall has made only modest progress. Some societies, including Brazil, Mexico and Chile, have made distinct improvements in average living standards, although economic inequality remains very high. Within Africa there are clear contrasts between different countries, but on average the continent has suffered a disastrous relative decline – and in some parts, an absolute decline – in income and living standards. The population of sub-Saharan Africa is expanding faster that that of any other region in the world. It has the highest long-term debt as a proportion of GDP, over 80 per cent in 1999 compared to 40 per cent for Latin America in that year. Industrial production grew at a mere 0.2 per cent, compared to a 15 per cent increase in East Asia. The parlous state of Africa, however, has little or nothing to do with globalization – the continent has been largely excluded from some of the major globalizing trends. It is the result of its long history of colonialism, and the activities of the rival superpowers during the Cold War, coupled to internal strife and the ravages of disease.

To create a happier future for Africa will require much more help, material and non-material, from the wealthy countries than has been forthcoming so far. Yet without internal reform, such support can be only of limited value. Most of the difficulties that inhibit the development of impoverished countries, in Africa and elsewhere, don't come from the global economy, or from the self-seeking behaviour of rich nations. They lie inside the developing countries themselves, in the shape of authoritarian government, ethnic divisions, corruption, poorly developed civil society and the low level of emancipation of women. The list is daunting, but given sufficient political will and leadership, changes can be made even in societies where conditions seem quite unpropitious.

We know of only one way in which large numbers of people can be leveraged out of poverty in developing societies. It is not through redistribution. It is through economic development in which the poor participate. This process has not taken place in countries that have tried to separate themselves from the global economy, but only in those that have engaged with it. Those societies that have isolated themselves, such as Burma, or North Korea, are among the most impoverished in the world. For poorer countries everything depends upon the conditions of engagement with the world economy. The critics of globalization are right to say that this connection cannot happen simply through free market mechanisms. As the former chief economist of the World Bank, Joseph Stiglitz, has pointed out, there is no case of effective economic development, among richer or among poorer nations, in which government and the state have not been involved in a fairly central fashion.[48] Opening up the economy of a poor country to world markets without other conditions being right can easily impoverish it still further, as well as make it more unstable and vulnerable.

Stiglitz argues in effect for a third way in development strategy, and it is a perspective that fits well with the wider framework of New Labour. For some thirty years after the Second World War, he points out, it was widely thought that that the state, using development planning, should be the guiding force in development. This approach failed: the poor economic performance of China and India during the period bears witness to this fact. Later it became generally believed that, if the state couldn't do the job, we should go down the path of economic deregulation and free markets. But this tactic has been at most only partly successful. One of the most important lessons we have learned is how difficult it is for markets to become established. Governments have to deploy policies that go well beyond simply getting out of the way of the market, and help build the institutions without which markets can't function, including at a minimum effective laws and the legal institutions that can enforce them. Government and markets should be seen as complementary, not as substitutes. The regulation of financial institutions, support for education, the creation of infrastructure, the provision of technology, the direct alleviation of poverty – all entail substantial government involvement, as happened in successful development in East Asia.

7

Conclusion

When a goal is greatly desired, and has taken a long while to reach, achieving it may perversely leave one feeling hollow and unsatisfied. Something like this seems to have happened following the election of 2001, offering Labour its holy grail, the long-awaited full second term. Even among the party leadership, and certainly among many supporters, the reaction to the victory was restrained and hesitant rather than enthusiastic. There was little evidence of the mood of celebration that greeted the victory four years before.

A critical election?

Yet in truth not only was the 2001 election result a significant achievement, it has greater implications than may appear at first sight. One of the factors taking the gloss off of the event was the poor electoral turnout. Many claimed that the low figure signalled increasing political apathy and perhaps general disillusionment with New Labour. But studies carried out since the election do not bear out these assertions. Surveys do not show any increase in feelings of political disaffection since 1997. There is in fact little direct relationship between people's expressed interest in policies and participation. Of those who say they are uninterested in politics, 53 per cent still claim to have voted. Asked to respond to the statement 'I don't think voting is very important', 90 per cent disagreed.[49] Of those who did not participate more, if they had voted, would have supported Labour than would have voted for either of the other two big parties.[50] What happened was essentially a free rider effect. Many of those who stayed away from the polling booth did so because they saw the result as a foregone conclusion.

The 2001 poll may have been what political scientists call a 'critical election'. A critical election is one which signals a permanent change in voting habits – an alteration in patterns of political support. The numbers supporting the Tories have dropped, while the proportion aligned with Labour has stayed stable. The Tories' days as the natural party of government are over and might not return. During the heyday of Mrs Thatcher, it appeared that a majority of the electorate sympathized with her view of the world, with its mixture of narrow nationalism, anti-Europeanism and selfish individualism. The Tories based their election strategy upon such a presumption, but this approach was a fundamental mistake. Whatever may have been true a decade ago, the Thatcherite outlook now appeals only to a minority of voters and a dwindling minority at that. The country as a whole is more liberal and cosmopolitan in outlook, and more supportive of public services and the public provision of social benefits than many political observers believed.

New Labour is therefore in a strong position and should stay that way. The fate of political parties and coalitions is affected by many contingencies and unforeseen events. We should not substitute for the refrain of fifteen years ago 'How can Labour ever win again?' the reverse assumption: 'How can Labour ever lose?' Right-wing governments, after all, have been returned to power over recent years in a number of industrial countries, including the US, Italy, Spain, Austria and Norway.

Yet conservatism is in worse shape ideologically than the

centre-left. The events of 1989 proved even more disorienting for the right than for the left. One of the main unifying features of conservative philosophy, anti-communism, disappeared. Conservatives in most countries adopted free market philosophy, but it has proved a corrosive influence. Christian democracy, the leading form of conservatism in the EU states, has come under great pressure and in some countries has dissolved altogether.

Compassionate conservatism is an attempt to develop a new right-of-centre political philosophy, but it is ideologically weak and unconvincing. Instead of focusing only on Christianity, it emphasizes faith-based organizations in general as a means of delivering welfare and of creating social solidarity.[51] It proved a useful campaign label for the Republicans during the last US presidential election, but once in power they proceeded largely to ignore it. Caring conservatism might have a short life.

Labour's vision

It is often said that New Labour has no clear vision of the future, of what it stands for and what kind of society it wants to create. There is some validity in these accusations, but they can readily be countered. The following would be my version of how to do so. Labour today stands for a new progressivism, which aims to address the aspirations and needs of a wide constituency of the population. The new progressivism stands firmly in the traditions of social democracy – it *is* social democracy, brought up to date and made relevant to a rapidly changing world. As a social democratic party, New Labour must seek to defend and revitalize public institutions and the public sphere. This aim demands strong and active government, required to advance the public interest. In a differentiated and complex world, the reinvigoration of government at the national level must be accompanied by devolution and an expansion of regional and local democratic power. Modern government is a matter of 'multilayered governance'. Governance has to stretch above the level of the nation as well as below, since many of our problems cannot be dealt with only at the national level.

Government needs to modernize and reform the state, including the welfare state, to cope with new demands, expectations and risks. A developed welfare state, providing a variety of resources and social protection, is as essential today as it was in previous generations. But some forms and aspects of traditional welfare systems need substantial change if they are to deliver the public goods citizens want. The state cannot provide public services efficiently and equitably without collaborating with non-state agencies, including non-profit organizations, third sector groups and private companies.

Social justice and economic competitiveness should not be treated as though they were distinct and separate from one another. A competitive economy, in which the workforce is able to adapt to regular technological innovation, is the necessary condition of job creation and the goal of sustaining full employment. Achieving a high level of employment – a high employment ratio – is important both for combating poverty and for the provision of other public goods. A high employment ratio should go along with a good minimum wage and other forms of labour protection. However, these have to be skewed towards human capital guarantees rather than passive benefits.

Mrs Thatcher's communications guru, Maurice Saatchi, once said that Tories are 'cruel and efficient', while Labour is 'caring and incompetent'. But New Labour has shown that it is possible to be both caring and competent. Indeed, the one is the condition of the other, as the disintegration of and loss of popular support for conservatism show. Sound economic management is not only essential for prosperity, it is the key to the revival of public services and the cultivation of a thriving civil society.

New Labour is a modernizing party. Modernization is not a meaningless term. It refers to the need to reshape the institutions of the country to respond to changes that are transforming the economy, sovereignty, cultural life, and the wider international system. There is a crucial connection between economic prosperity and a cosmopolitan, outward-looking society. Multiculturalism and cosmopolitanism find their counterpart in an internationalist outlook, given concrete form in Europe in the shape of the European Union. Like domestic institutions, the EU cannot be taken as a given, but needs reform and modernization, processes which Britain should look to influence in a direct and central way.

Within the UK decentralization and the devolution of power can release local energy and initiative, as well as enhance local democracy. This vision is a pluralist one, but does not endorse the primacy of identity politics. Britain is, and should remain, a unitary society. Tolerance of multiple identity, and of cultural difference, should be actively promoted within such a social order. Our society should become simultaneously more egalitarian and more meritocratic, the one again being a condition of the other.

Cosmopolitanism cannot apply only at the cultural and social levels. It must embrace political philosophy too. This observation brings us back to the attitudes I mentioned at the beginning and the need to break away from them. If we wish to overcome our insularity economically and culturally, we must do so at the level of political debate as well.

Notes

1 John Lloyd, 'How New Labour wrestled with a world it never made', *New Statesman*, 30 Apr. 2001, p. 9.
2 Tony Blair, 'Third Way, Phase Two', *Prospect*, March 2001, pp. 10–13. Polly Toynbee, 'This is Blair's new road map, but it leads nowhere', *Guardian*, 28 Feb. 2001.
3 Wolfgang Merkel, 'The third ways of social democracy', in Anthony Giddens (ed.), *The Global Third Way Debate* (Cambridge: Polity, 2001).
4 Richard Gillespie, 'A programme for social democratic revival?', in Richard Gillespie and William E. Paterson, *Rethinking Social Democracy in Western Europe* (London: Cass, 1993), p. 175.
5 René Cuperus and Johannes Kandel, 'The magical return of social democracy: an introduction', in *European Social Democracy: Transformation and Progress* (Amsterdam: Ebert Foundation, 1998).
6 Kenneth S. Baer, *Reinventing Democrats: The Politics of Liberalism from Reagan to Clinton* (Lawrence: University Press of Kansas, 2000), p. 2.
7 Roy Hattersley, 'It's no longer my party', *Guardian*, 24 June 2001.
8 Gøsta Esping-Anderson, 'A welfare state for the twenty-first century', in Giddens, *The Global Third Way Debate*.
9 Ted Halstead and Michael Lind, *The Radical Centre* (New York: Doubleday, 2001).
10 Ibid., pp. 4–6.

Notes

11 Dick Morris, *The New Prince* (Los Angeles: Renaissance Books, 1999).

12 Donald Sassoon, 'Convergence, continuity and change on the European left', in Gavin Kelly (ed.), *The New European Left* (London: Fabian Society, 1999).

13 David Marquand, 'A philosophy that would not die', *New Statesman*, 26 Feb. 1999, p. 25.

14 Will Hutton, *The State We're In* (London: Jonathan Cape, 1995); *The State to Come* (London: Vintage, 1997); *The Stakeholding Society* (Cambridge: Polity, 1999).

15 Fritz Scharpf, 'Employment and the welfare state in the open economy', in René Cuperus, Karl Duffek and Johannes Kandel, *Multiple Third Ways* (Amsterdam: Ebert Foundation, 2001). See also Fritz W. Scharpf and Vivien A. Schmidt, *Welfare and Work in the Open Economy* (Oxford: Oxford University Press, 2001).

16 Fabian Society, *Paying for Progress: A New Politics of Tax for Public Spending* (London: Fabian Society, 2000). The book does nevertheless make many important contributions, for example, offering proposals on 'reconnecting' citizens to their taxes by increasing their transparency.

17 See, for instance, Polly Toynbee and David Walker, *Did Things Get Better?* (London: Penguin, 2001).

18 'Fiscal reforms since May 1997', Institute for Fiscal Studies (IFS), London, 2001.

19 Labour Party Manifesto: *New Labour: Because Britain Deserves Better* (London: Labour Party, 1997).

20 Tony Blair, 'The government's agenda for the future', transcript of speech given on 8 Feb. 2001, p. 2.

21 Carl Emmerson and Christine Frayne: *Overall Tax and Spending.* (London: Institute for Fiscal Studies, Apr. 2001, p. 2). The government's official figure for taxation as a proportion of GDP is lower, but the IFS's calculation conforms more closely to international accounting conventions.

22 Adair Turner, *Just Capital* (London: Macmillan, 2001).

Notes

23 Suggested in the Fabian volume; see Fabian Society, *Paying for Progress*.

24 Philip Gould, *The Unfinished Revolution* (London: Abacus, 1999), p. 232.

25 Amartya Sen, *Inequality Reexamined* (Oxford: Clarendon Press, 1992).

26 The Sutton Trust, *Educational Apartheid: A Practical Way Forward* (London: Sutton Trust, 2001).

27 Department of the Environment, Transport and the Regions, *Government Response to the Report of the Joint Committee on the Draft Local Government (Organisation and Standards) Bill* (London: HMSO, 2000), p. 10.

28 Constitution Unit, *Monitor*, no. 16 (Sept. 2001), p. 9.

29 John Tomaney, 'New Labour and the English question', *Political Quarterly*, 70, no. 1 (1999), pp. 75–82, at p. 80.

30 Centro de Investigaciones Sociológicas (CIS), Madrid, 1997.

31 Anthony Giddens, *The Third Way* (Cambridge: Polity, 1998).

32 Turner, *Just Capital*, ch. 9.

33 Albert Weale, *The New Politics of Pollution* (Manchester: Manchester University Press, 1992), p. 78.

34 David Gibbs, 'Ecological modernisation, economic development and regional development agencies', *Geoforum*, 31 (2000).

35 Jonathan Fenby, *France on the Brink* (New York: Arcade, 1999).

36 Nicholas Timmins, 'Squaring circles': funding the provision of public services', *Political Quarterly*, 72 (2001).

37 Christopher Hood, 'Contemporary public management: a new global paradigm?', *Public Policy and Administration*, 10 (1995).

38 HM Treasury, *Public Private Partnerships* (London: HMSO, 2000), p. 12.

39 Ibid., p. 8.

40 OECD, *Integrating Transport in the City* (Paris: OECD, 2000), p. 43

41 Paul A. Grout, 'The economics of the private finance initiative', *Oxford Review of Economic Policy*, 13 (1997). See also the Institute

Notes

for Public Policy Research, *Building Better Partnerships*. London: IPPR, 2001, pp. 77–103. This report is the best and most exhaustive study of PPPs in the UK produced to date, and rightly has been widely debated.

42 Martin Summers, 'Only connect: towards a new democratic settlement', in Mark Perryman, *The Blair Agenda* (London: Lawrence and Wishart, 1996).

43 Michael Brereton and Michael Temple, 'The new public service ethos', *Public Administration*, 77 (1999).

44 Ed Mayo and Henrietta Moore, *The Mutual State* (London: New Economics Foundation, 2001).

45 Anthony Giddens, *Runaway World* (London: Profile Books, 1999).

46 Mary Kaldor, *Old and New Wars* (Cambridge: Polity, 1999).

47 Glenn Firebaugh, 'Empirics of world income inequality', *American Journal of Sociology*, 104 (1999).

48 Joseph Stiglitz, 'An agenda for development for the twenty-first century', in Giddens, *The Global Third Way Debate*.

49 Constitution Unit, *Monitor*, no. 16 (Sept. 2001), p. 6.

50 Robert Worcester and Roger Mortimore, *Explaining Labour's Second Landslide* (London: Politico's Publishing, 2001), ch. 2.

51 Marvin Olasky, *Compassionate Conservatism* (New York: Free Press, 2000).

LITTAUER LIBRARY
＊ NORTH YARD
HARVARD UNIVERSITY

THE BORROWER WILL BE CHARGED
AN OVERDUE FEE IF THIS BOOK IS
NOT RETURNED TO THE LIBRARY ON
OR BEFORE THE LAST DATE STAMPED
BELOW. NON-RECEIPT OF OVERDUE
NOTICES DOES NOT EXEMPT THE
BORROWER FROM OVERDUE FEES.

Harvard College Littauer Library
Cambridge, MA 02138 (617) 495-2560